An Econometric Model
of Residential Location

An Econometric Model of Residential Location

Michael Granfield
UCLA

Ballinger Publishing Company ● Cambridge, Mass.
A Subsidiary of J. B. Lippincott Company

This book is printed on recycled paper.

International Standard Book Number: 0–88410–410–9

Library of Congress Catalog Card Number: 75–2246

Printed in the United States of America

Library of Congress Cataloging in Publication Data

Granfield, Michael.
    An econometric model of residential location.

Bibliography: p.
1. Residential mobility–Buffalo–Mathematical models. 2. Residential mobility–Milwaukee–Mathematical models. I. Title.
HD7287.5.G65   301.5'4   75–2246
ISBN 0–88410–410–9

Contents

v

List of Figures

List of Tables

An Econometric Model
of Residential Location

Chapter One

Introduction

Since the early 1950s, location theorists and practitioners have been exposed to a number of empirical works analyzing the determinants of residential location both on an individual as well as on an aggregate household level. These studies have employed a variety of methodologies varying from simple linear regression models to more complex constructs such as gravity and linear programming models requiring iterative solutions. The urban areas examined have been equally diverse from large Midwest cities (e.g., Detroit and Chicago) to smaller Southern cities (e.g., Greensboro and Raleigh, North Carolina). These diverse methodologies and empirical data bases make it difficult to abstract many regularities or consistent predictions of broad applicability with respect to residential location behavior.

The difficulties of developing general statements about residential location behavior stem from two main sources (other than the more obvious ones of simple compatibility and data homogeneity that have already been enumerated):

1. The tendency to develop ever more complex methodoligical techniques that are too sophisticated for present data sources, which leads to the generation of data proxies (which are not totally valid proxies) or the creation of non-operational and non-predictive models;
2. The use of aggregate data due to the necessity of reporting "good fitting" models where aggregation hides the great variations in individual household behavior on either an intra- or inter-urban level.

This study of residential location seeks to overcome some of these difficulties by employing present data sources to their practical limit and avoiding the creation of excessive proxies. In analyzing residential location, the study utilizes a simple, three-equation, linear, multivariate recursive model to

3

determine where households would want to locate and the type of residence they would want to inhabit. It contrasts these aspects with the available supply of desired housing in a given area and makes the required allocational adjustments employing simulation via an adjustment algorithm. Thus, the study takes an economic approach to the residential location problem by explicitly viewing the process as one of the interaction of the forces of demand and supply for scarce sites.

THE DEMAND PORTION OF THE LOCATIONAL MODEL

The demand portion of the overall locational model views residential location as a sequential process involving three, distinct, recursive stages. In the first stage, the household determines its housing budget constraint or, in other words, the amount it desires to spend annually on housing. This decision is formulated as a multi-dimensional consumption function in which annual housing expenditures (CH) are viewed as a function of current income (Y), neighborhood median income (YN), and occupation (OCCUP) or in functional form, CH = FN (Y, YN, OCCUP).

Having determined its budget constraint, the household next examines potential locations for its residence. The critical variables affecting the locational decision in this model are (1) the budget constraint (CH), which determines the basic neighborhoods in which search can take place; (2) the ethnic race of the household (RACE), which if non-white may act as a further constraint on alternative residential sites; (3) neighborhood median income (YN), which is a proxy for income class clustering (i.e., above and beyond the income constraint, people with similar incomes may desire to live together due to familiarity, similar amenity desires and so forth; (4) accessibility (ACCTY) to work expressed as a time–cost factor (combination of commuter time[1] and income), which reflects the fact that the higher one's income, the greater is the opportunity cost of commuter travel; and (5) the model of travel (MODE), one uses to get to work, with the use of a car permitting more mobility and hence a wider latitude in selecting a residence site. Thus, LOCH = FN(CH, YN, RACE, ACCTY, MODE).

Having determined a general location for the residence, the household then turns its attention to selecting the type (i.e., single-family, two-family, multi-family) of home or rental unit (TYPR) it will ultimately occupy. TYPR is, in turn, a function of the household's budget constraint, the predetermined *area* of residence choice (i.e., how the surrounding environment affects their choice), and the size of the family (SZF). Thus, TYPR = FN(CH, LOCH, SZF).

SUPPLY CONSTRAINT

In order to properly simulate a real market environment, it was necessary to construct a supply constraint for the households to reflect the fact that all households would not locate where they most desired—that is, another household would outbid them for the desired site necessitating a readjustment. Ideally, the supply constraint should have reflected such variables as the opportunity costs of various sites, reservation prices of current homeowners, property taxes, and so forth. However, since such information was not available, a linear supply constraint function for each type of dwelling for each area was constructed. The three independent variables employed were population density, accessibility to the area, and total area employment [note: other variables such as zoning restrictions were tried but were not statistically significant].

ANALYSIS AND SIMULATIONS

Both the estimated results on the parameters of the models as well as the policy simulations yielded some very interesting conclusions. With regard to the model itself, the demand portion produced the more dramatic findings. Among these, for example, were (1) socio-economic variables such as ethnic race and neighborhood income structure seem to have replaced location of one's work place (or accessibility to it) as the most crucial variables affecting residential location; (2) suburbanites apparently have a significantly different locational function than city dwellers (either white or non-white), which implies that suburbanites are not simply richer or younger city dwellers but rather a group with a quite different preference function for location; and (3) current income was more critical in affecting current housing expenditures for whites than non-whites, which seems to cast some doubt on the generalization that non-whites have a relatively higher discount rate.

In terms of the policy simulations, the conclusions were (1) strict enforcement of open occupancy laws was seen to be more important than income supplements in changing racial housing patterns although there are some important qualifications to this recommendation; (2) for some cities, the flight to the suburbs may dramatically slow down whereas the density of their outer municipal areas will rise to absorb the increased migration from the center city; and (3) freeways may have considerably less effect, in the future, on residential location patterns due to the decline in importance of work accessibility.

Chapter Two

Urban Model Building

This chapter deals with the process of urban model building and the general nature of urban models. The purpose of urban models is to aid both the decision maker and the social scientist in predicting and analyzing complex urban processes. The current vehicles for both analysis and prediction are quantitative urban models that are mathematical in nature and often use the computer as a requisite computational device. In discussing the nature of such models one must be very careful to distinguish in exactly what sense one is discussing their content and purpose.

In general, these models are a representation of reality, and therefore the act of setting forth such a model represents a commitment to some sort of theory. In this connection, the model is usually designed to correspond with some conception of reality as the modeler perceives it. An alternative application of the term model can occur in connection with the purely mathematical formulation of the model that does not correspond to any explicit theory in its content. Thus, some people speak of linear programming and dynamic programming models or of a linear regression model with the main emphasis on the mathematical structure of the model that seemingly exists independently of the variables and constraints. In this context, it is important to note that a model must be of something and that its form is secondary although usually connected with the purpose of the model. In short, a model is an experimental design based on a theory whose actual form is not essential to the theory, but which facilitates the quantifying and testing of the theory itself.[1] This particular approach emphasizes two aspects of models that are important: "First, it stresses the connection between models and theories while at the same time admitting that models are frequently truncated theories, sacrificing richness and completeness for operational purposes. Second, the definition emphasizes the experimental means of relating theory to the real world."[2]

Thus, after having briefly discussed the nature of a model and its purpose, the next step is to classify the different forms that models may take and the subsequent implications and purposes of these particular forms.

CLASSIFYING URBAN MODELS

One means of classifying urban models is to contrast descriptive versus analytic models. Analytic models, by definition, make explicit statements about cause and effect, which are quite specific and which are possibly testable at both the aggregated macro level and the micro level. Descriptive models, on the other hand, do not assert any particular theory, but rather seek out regularities in relationships with the eventual aim of postulating a theory based on them. The difficulties connected with constructing an analytic model to explain urban phenomena are the complete information demands for the construction of adequate models—that is, many analytic models have been forced to lump so many factors in their "ceteris paribus" assumption that their results are either trivial or deceiving in that they predict directional changes that are not only effected by what is omitted but also are overwhelmed by their ommissions. Consequently, model builders may attempt to affect a compromise by including certain stable and predictable analytic relationships that are supplemented by less precise descriptive relationships.

Another dimension in model building concerns the difference between holistic and partial models. Holistic models attempt to take in all factors that affect the model. For example, a model of urban economy would include variables or submodels for population, rate of employment, income, and so forth, which would then dynamically interact to simulate the actual workings of an urban economy. A partial model would only examine one of these variables or submodels and would hold all others constant. A holistic model seemingly could be created by combining various partial models; but in actuality this becomes a more complex problem than one of elementary combination. This is because the actual communication between subsystems is probably much more complex and diverse than at first appears to be the case. In addition, the designation of the particular partial models must insure a certain degree of realism and interdependence that may conflict with what is easiest to examine in a partial framework.[3]

A parallel issue is the decision whether to adopt a micro or macro framework. This particular issue is a very perplexing one since macro relations are easier to analyze and predict (in an urban environment) but at times fail to accurately reflect or predict the micro phenomenon they are attempting to analyze on the aggregate level due to the inherent complexity of the examined phenomena. However, due to the newness of urban research, it is often only the aggregates that are of interest, and it is argued by some that this is where the emphasis should remain (at least temporarily). The reasoning underlying this position is that the data requirements for a rigorous micro analytic model are rarely met and that the manipulation of aggregate data to meet micro specifications can prove to be counterproductive and perhaps unsound.[4] Despite the paucity of present urban data, it is only with micro analytic models that we can hope to truly analyze and understand the inner workings of our urban environment and thus prescribe policies that will produce more useful results than now exist. Such micro models will also give some indication as to what variables should be examined (and data collected on) and to those that can be safely ignored.

If the model is to reflect urban phenomena accurately, the necessity of dynamic rather than static equilibrium models becomes apparent. In creating dynamic models, though, one must be careful to construct models whose key variables interact with time and are continuously dependent on the changes in time for their value rather than simply building a model that exogenously changes or inserts different values of certain variables as they change over time. In addition to the methodological problem of creating truly dynamic models, there exists the practical problem of poor or nonexistent time series data for urban variables. In the interim, while we await more adequate data, we will have to be satisfied with static equilibrium models that make full use of present theory and data. Whether the conclusions reached by these models will be rewarding, trivial, or even deceitful cannot in general be predetermined and will have to be judged on such weaker criteria as inherent logic and internal consistency.

Due to the uncertain nature of urban phenomena, some model builders feel that their models must be probabilistic to reflect this fact. One may debate the merits of consciously introducing uncertainty into a model whose exact specifications are by nature uncertain. In fact, there are some who regard such effects as wasteful and counterproductive except in certain limiting cases.[5] The dominant trend, then, in urban models continues to be a deterministic one, which seems to create enough uncertainty and conflict due to the empty and often disparate conclusions arrived at by such models. This seems to indicate that the science of urban model building has not yet reached a sophisticated enough stage to consciously begin introducing stochastic elements into the model.

A MARKET-ORIENTED CLASSIFICATION

So far urban models have been examined from an operational and methodological viewpoint. There are other and perhaps more fruitful ways to examine and generalize about urban models. Ira Lowry published a paper in which he examines seven urban models for their structural similarities. He does this by relating them through a generally accepted theory of the market for urban land.

To quote Lowry:

> Urban spatial organization is the outcome of a process which allo-
> cates activities to sites. In our society, the process is mainly one of
> transactions between owners of real estate and those who wish to
> rent or purchase space for their homes and businesses. These transac-
> tions are freely entered contracts, neither party having a legal obliga-
> tion to accept the other's offer. These elements suffice to define a
> "market" in the economists dictionary.

In short, there is a market for urban land, and the price of any
segment is determined by the interacting forces of supply and demand. The
demand by an establishment (either firm or household) for a particular site is a
function of many variables and can be viewed mathematically as: $P_{hi} = f(X_1^h \ h,$
$X_2^h, X_3^h \ - - - - -, Y_1^i, Y_2^i, h = 1, 2, - - - n)$. Here h is a particular establishment and
i is a particular site with the price P that establishment h will offer for site i
depending on a number of characteristics of the establishment (the Xs), and on a
number of characteristics of the site (the Ys) and so on. A similar function could
be developed for determining supply price. One can also derive an investment
function which owners use to evaluate the merits of site-improvements of the
form: $E_j^i = g(C_j^i, P;)$. In this notation, i is a specific site and j is a specific bundle
of site characteristics (i.e., some combination of the Ys that we encountered in
the evaluation function). E_j^i is the expected gain from converting site i to condition j. C_j^i is the expected cost of imposing the jth bundle of site characteristics
on site i, a cost which may well vary with the present condition of the site. P_j is
the current market price of sites in condition j. The owner will choose an
investment program which maximizes E_j^i. To do so, he must compare P_j and C_j^i
for each alternative j. To this function (or added into the cost function), it
would be necessary to add either a reaction function or probability function,
which would take into consideration the large externalities associated with site
improvement (i.e., it does very little good for one site to improve if other
neighboring sites do not improve or even deteriorate).[7]

The final equilibrium locations (in any given time period) of the
interacting supply and demand functions for each given parcel of land can be
usefully illustrated by means of a paradigm (see Figure 2-1).[8] Each square
represents a parcel of land that can be described horizontally by means of its
activity involvement (e.g., retailing, residential living, and so forth) or vertically
by its location in a given district. If an event occurs and causes an establishment
to move, this too can be represented by comparing an initial and terminal
location.

Since urban models are confronted with phenomena that are difficult to completely replicate either statically or dynamically, we will attempt to
stimulate one aspect of the paradigm while implicitly trying to simulate the

Figure 2–1. The Urban Land Market.

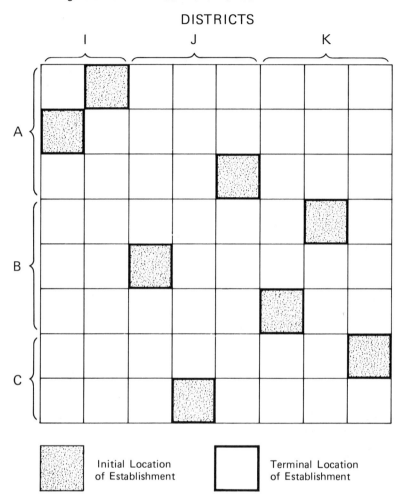

DISTRICTS

whole thing. Those models that emphasize the columns of the paradigm are known as land-use models, whereas those that emphasize the rows are location models. If, on the other hand, the emphasis is placed on movements within the paradigm, vertical movement models are land-use succession models and horizontal movement models are models of migration.[9] It should also be noted that some models cannot be placed in any of these four categories because they are either hybirds or cannot be meaningfully categorized at all. The usefullness of a particular approach of a model depends on the purpose of the model acting in conjunction with the available data. This particular thesis is locational in nature with migratory simulations.

Figure 2–2. Changes in Location and Land Use during a Transaction Period.

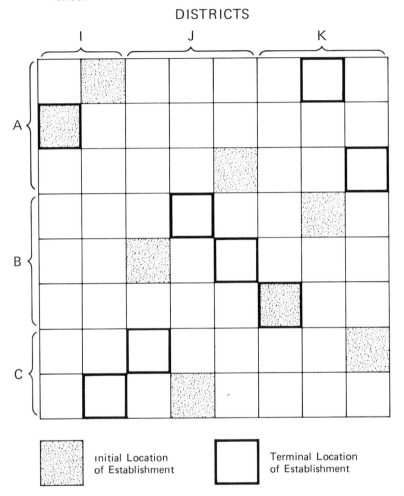

DISTRICTS

Initial Location of Establishment

Terminal Location of Establishment

To retrace somewhat, the location and activity involvement classifications can be seen as entering into the demand function (for any given period and for any given parcel of land) with the supply function being a simple constraint represented by the size of the paradigm. However, as one progresses from one period to the next the true nature of each parcel becomes apparent. Both the district and the potential activity involvement enter into both the supply and demand functions. This concept is very essential to the understanding of land markets and land succession and can best be illustrated by Figure 2–2.[10]

Although the paradigm and market approach may appear over-simplified to some, it is helpful in that it points out, in general, the workings of the urban land market and also gives a convenient reference point with which to gauge urban models that are capable of obscuring (in their workings and formulation) even their own modest or heroic aims.[11] Further, it enables the viewer to evaluate the model from a market criterion (not always the only criterion) by asking such questions as: How well *should* it work considering those aspects of the market process which are ignored or subordinated in the model's structure? Suppose the model were provided with accurate data and the parameters were fitted by exemplory statistical procedures, would it capture enough of the structure of the market to reproduce market results? Do the relationships that form the structure of the model appear to be consistent with market theory even if in crude detail? If some pertinent factors are not explicitly present as variables, can we believe that they are implicitly represented by fitted parameters that are fixed over time? Is the accounting system sufficiently rigorous to guaranteed internal consistency of the model's solution?[12]

If these questions cannot be answered affirmatively, then there is at least one crucial criterion that the model has failed to satisfy, which may lead us to reject it entirely depending on the importance placed on market credibility.

A SUBJECT-ORIENTED CLASSIFICATION SCHEME

A group of MBA's at Harvard have also attempted to cast urban models into an overall conceptical framework consisting of such elements as the subject, function, theory and method of the models:

> Roughly speaking, the subject of the model is the entity, or activity, that is projected, allocated, or manipulated by the model. The function of an urban planning model is to project or allocate the subject, or to derive new subjects. The theory of the model is the set of relationships, stated, or implied that is assumed to prevail between the subject of the model and the larger environment. The method is the mathematical form used to carry out the projection, allocation, or derivation.[13]

Thus, the subject matter of urban models can be divided into four classes: (1) land use, (2) economic activity, (3) population, and (4) transportation. The model is developed to analyze these phenomena with the eventual aim of understanding their workings enough to make meaningful projections of their future behavior.

> Urban planning models perform three functions: (1) they project the subject, (2) they allocate the subject, (3) they derive one subject from another. Whatever the subject may be, the model's purpose is

either to estimate the future of the subject (projection), or to divide the subject into subsets (allocation), or to transform the subject by deriving another subject from it (derivation). Most models perform two or more of these functions in varying combinations. A model may, for example, project the subject into the future and then allocate it to subsets of activity; or a model may allocate a subject, project its subsets into the future, and then use these subsets to devise a new subject.[14]

The theory of an urban model is the set of assumptions and relationships which express the models content and reveal its purpose. In other words, the underlying theory of an urban planning model is the set of relationships, stated or implied, between the subject of the model and the larger environment. It is impossible to make a theoryless model (not entirely or necessarily true), for either the model derives directly from theory as a symbolic statement of it, or it abstracts phenomena to symbolic form and relates these structurally, thus creating theory. Models are either theory based or theory laden.[15]

The operational method of the model is simply the technique that the model uses to perform its assigned task and may be econometric, mathematical or simulative in form (or a combination of these).

In summary, three general classifying schemes that could be used in the analysis of urban models have been presented. The first and last deal with describing the model and its methodology, the second (Lowry's) deals more with the workings or predictions of the models. To the extent that we do not have an "optimum" form for an urban model, Lowry's emphasis on performance may well be the one meaningful classification—that is, are models useful as predictive tools as well as accurate reflections of urban phenomena or are they merely methodological artifacts valued for their form rather than their content or usefulness?

Chapter Three

Two Urban Models

The three general frameworks within which one can analyze urban models having been presented in Chapter Two, the task in this chapter becomes one of examining particular urban models in somewhat more depth. Rather than make a cursory review of the many urban models that have been developed, we examine only two models in depth. These highlight the two particular extremes that urban models may take, namely, the analytic and the descriptive.

The analytic model that is examined is one that was developed by William Alonso. It concentrates on residential location although its approach is extended to explain retail and manufacturing location (with the requisite change in parameters).[1] In contrast to this approach, Ira Lowry developed a descriptive model (based on a gravity model) of the Pittsburgh area (using traffic data) to explain residential and retail location with manufacturing location and employment as the exogeneous variables.[2]

THE ALONSO MODEL

In examining Alonso's model, it is essential to examine his assumptions and their implications since it is these assumptions that produce both the rigor and neatness of the model as well as indicating its potential weaknesses.

Alonso's major assumptions are:

1. Perfect knowledge on the part of the consumer;
2. Freely mobile land market;
3. All land is of equal quality;
4. Single market and employment center.[3]

In deriving a demand surface or curve for the residential consumer, Alonso begins by presenting a household budget equation and then manipulating

15

and applying this equation to produce the demand curve. The budgetary equation is:

$$Y = P_z z + P(t) q + k(t); \qquad (1)$$

Y = household income;

P_z = price of the composite good, reflecting all other goods;

z = quantity of the composite good;

$P(t)$ = price of land at distance t from the center of the city;

q = quantity of land consumed;

$k(t)$ = commuting costs to distance t;

t = distance to center of the city.[4]

A complete graphical exposition of this equation would, of necessity, be in three dimensions but by holding one variable constant, we can examine the relationship between the remaining two in two dimensional space. Let us begin by holding t constant at $t = t_o$ and examine the relationship between q and z (see Figure 3–1). This is a linear relationship that indicates the trade-off between q and z as a function of their respective prices. Next, let us hold the composite good constant at $z = z_o$ and examine the relationship (see Figure 3–2) between q and t, which is non-linear as it indicates that as t increases the price of land decreases (producing larger q), but that this cost saving is eventually offset by a more than commensurate rise in commuting costs.

Finally, let us hold q constant at $q = q_o$ and allow t and z to vary, which produces a result very similar to the previous one due to the fact that increasing commuting costs eventually outweigh the decreasing cost of the constant amount of land (see Figure 3–3). When combined, these three curves yield a locus of opportunities that indicates the simultaneous trade-offs between location, land consumed, and commuting costs a residential locator makes in selecting a site.[5]

In order to derive a demand surface, we must combine the locus of opportunities surface with an indifference surface. The derivation of the indifference surface will parallel that used in deriving the locus of opportunities surface. First, hold t constant and allow q and z to vary, which yields the normal indifference curve (see Figure 3–4) indicating that the residential locator will give up more of the composite good to obtain more land (actual rate depends on MRTS between the two). Secondly, if we hold z constant at $z = z_o$ the relationship between q and t is revealed (see Figure 3–5), which indicates that as t increases one must have more and more land to consume to remain at the same level of satisfaction (i.e., t has negative utility). Thirdly, if we hold q constant at $q = q_o$ a similar result is produced (see Figure 3–6) for z and t. The area of

Figure 3–1. Trade-off between Land and Composite Good.

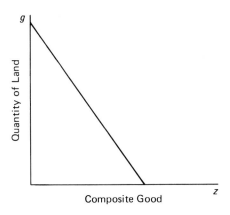

Figure 3–2. Trade-off between Land and Accessibility.

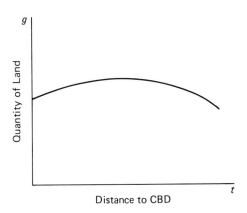

Figure 3–3. Trade-off between Composite Good and Accessibility.

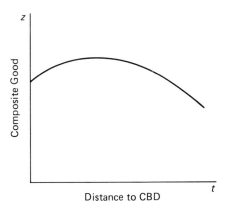

Figure 3–4.   Preference Function for Land and Composite Good.

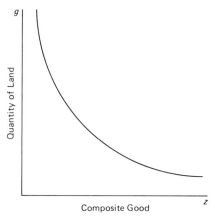

Figure 3–5.   Preference Function for Land and Accessibility.

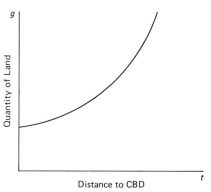

Figure 3–6.   Preference Function for Composite Good and Accessibility.

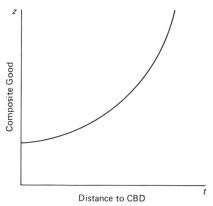

tangency between the indifference surface (produced by these three curves) and the locus of opportunities surface yields the demand surface for the residential locator.[6]

This final derivation of a demand surface can be shown more succinctly and perhaps more rigorously by using the mathematical technique of the Lagrange multiplier. In addition to the budget equation, there is a utility function or equation of the form: $u = u(z, q, t)$. When these two are combined into a Lagrangean function, we get:

$$L = u(z, q, t) - (p_z z + P(t) q + k(t) - y).$$

When the object is to maximize utility subject to the budget constraint, we get the following:

$$\frac{\partial L}{\partial Z} = U_z - P_z = 0; \tag{2}$$

$$\frac{\partial L}{\partial q} = U_q - P(t) = 0; \tag{3}$$

$$\frac{\partial L}{\partial t} = U_t - \lambda [P'(t) q + k'(t)] = 0; \tag{4}$$

$$\frac{\partial L}{\partial \lambda} = P_z Z + P(t) q + k(t) = Y. \tag{5}$$

It is important to note that these are only first order (necessary) conditions for maximization, but even these reveal some interesting results. For example, by combining equations (2) and (3) one arrives at the following result:

$$U_z - P_z = U_q - P(t), \tag{2}$$

$$\frac{U_z}{U_q} = \frac{P_z}{P_t} \text{, or alternatively} \tag{6}$$

$$\frac{U_z}{P_z} = \frac{U_q}{P_t} \tag{7}$$

Equation (6) tells us that in equilibrium, when consumer resources are allocated efficiently, the ratio of marginal utilities produced by the consumption of land (i.e., services from it) and the composite good must equal the ratio of their respective prices. Equation (7) tells us much the same thing but perhaps in a clearer manner—that is, it indicates that the marginal utility per dollar spent must be, in consumer equilibrium, the same for land as for the composite good. If we further disaggregate z into its component parts, we arrive at the general conclusion that the marginal utility per dollar spent, in consumer equilibrium, must be the same for all goods and services consumed. By solving equations (4), (5), and (6) simultaneously, we obtain the individual's optimal combinations of the three unknowns z, q, and t. The unique combination of z, q, and t that the consumer will actually purchase depends on where this demand surface intersects the market supply surface, which yields the final market equilibrium solution.[a]

In constructing the final market solution, Alonso transforms the demand surface derived above into a bid price function and further derives a supply function that maximizes revenue to the suppliers. The final solution here is very similar to Lowry's "Seven Models . . ." in that all firms and households bid for a parcel of land and it goes to the bidder with the highest offered price (which guarantees the satisfaction of the supply equation also). However, despite the superior elegance of this approach, it still preserves the essential assumptions and workings that have already been examined, which are also the essential elements to be criticized in Alonso's approach. Within this context there are two major flaws in Alonso's approach. First, when he assumes all land is of equal quality, he dismisses the category of amenities of both a social and physical nature, which would affect the demand function or surface—that is, he dismisses the existence of racial and ethnic ghettos on the social side and the locational advantages of good schools, streets, garbage collection, and so forth, on the physical side. Secondly, his fourth assumption of a single market and employment center implies a concentric theory of development.[7]

Of course, whenever one examines a complex social and economic phenomenon such as residential location, it is necessary to use the familiar tool of "ceteris paribus" and examine only those few variables that will best illuminate the inner workings and direction of the examined phenomenon. The breakdown in this approach occurs when what is omitted is of greater importance (both in direction and magnitude) than what is included. Sometimes this particular error can be determined "a priori" due to a logical inconsistency in the model or by the irrational or incredible information yielded or predicted by the model. This is not the case with Alonso's model as it is quite consistent, is analytically thorough, and predicts a pattern of land values and land consumption (i.e., land values decline as one moves farther away from CBD; and the consumer purchases more land as the distance from CBD increases) that are consistent with empirical observation and common sense. Therefore, any

---

a. Second order conditions would dictate, for a maximum, that the second total derivative of the Lagrangean function be less than zero, which would imply that the indifference function be convex.

attempt to refute the theory must postulate different assumptions that are as adequate as Alonso's and follow them up with empirical verification. Since Alonso would readily admit to the flaws in assumption four, the task becomes essentially one of examining the importance of amenities in a theoretical and empirical framework. This, in fact, is what this study partially attempts to do. However, before launching into it, let us examine the findings of other authors that tend to support or refute Alonso's approach.

RESIDENTIAL LOCATION AS SEEN BY OTHERS

Lowdon Wingo uses an approach very similar to Alonso's in that he presents the same trade-off between distance from work (not necessarily a single center of employment as it may be dispersed centers) and quantity of land demanded, but adds the more sophisticated tool of commuting costs as a function of the individual's income (i.e., time–cost based on income). His actual location mechanism is the identical one of a competitive bidding process.[8]

Richard Muth repeats the same general reasoning but adds the essential factor that income is the most important variable affecting the consumption for housing in a metropolitan area and that this in turn is negatively related to the density gradient.[9]

John F. Kain substantiates this by stating his central hypothesis: "Households substitute journey-to-work expenditures for site expenditures. This substitution depends primarily on household preferences for low density as opposed to high density residential services."[10] He further elaborates on this by making empirical studies of journey-to-work relationships in Chicago and Detroit, in which he found:

> With a few exceptions for the inntermost rings, the residence ring housing the largest proportion of each workplace rings workers is also the same ring in which they are employed. In short, workers tend to live in their workplace rings; furthermore, this tendency is greater for outer than inner workplace rings. This suggests that a tendency exists to try to economize on transportation outlays for worktrips and that this may be somewhat easier to achieve if one's workplace is at a distance from the CBD.[11]

Kain makes one further important point with regard to time rather than just distance, which is:

> While the difference in mean travel time by the five modes are small, the differences in mean distance traveled are large. In particular, if commuters use rail or automobile, they may travel nearly twice as far in only slightly more time than they would require by other modes.[12]

In summary, Kain's chief contribution has been to present empirical data that seem to indicate that people do tend to minimize the time it takes to get to work, which usually but not necessarily minimizes the journey-to-work distance variable. The economic rationale for this behavior is that "those using the more expensive transport modes (auto and rail), which do save time, have the largest families and travel farthest; apparently to secure economical housing of their choice."[13]

Beverly and Otis Dudley Duncan sought to explore the relationship between the pattern of location of industry in the city and the pattern of residential differentiation according to the industrial affiliations of the work force. They argue that the internal residential structure of cities reflects the industrial composition of their economic base and the locational determinants of the basic industries. In other words, the journey-to-work relationship would be a function of the type of employment being considered (e.g., machinists will locate vis-à-vis their workplace in a different manner than lawyers).[14]

> The implications of these results is that the residential pattern of an industry group is shaped by the locational pattern of the industry, the occupational composition of its work force, and the residential pattern of the several occupational groups. Any model which sought to account for the residential patterns of industry groups solely on the basis on the differentiation of the city by socioeconomic level would be demonstrably deficient.[15]

Thus, the Duncan's felt that their model should account for the residential pattern of an industry within the metropolitan district or more specifically the area variation in the proportion of the resident labor force employed in a particular industry. Two probable determinants of residential patterns were identified: (1) inter-area differences in accessibility to the industry's workplaces; and (2) inter-area differences in socioeconomic status (occupations composition). The model assumed that the proportion of the resident work force in a particular industry is a function of the industry's relative potential (i.e., relative accessibility to its workplaces) and the expected proportion of residents in the industry (i.e., socioeconomic status).[16] Therefore, another qualifying factor, that of occupational composition, has been added to the analysis of residential location.

Richard Muth has examined and attempted to explain the decline in the rent gradient for land (or density gradient) as distance from the CBD increases. One explanation is that "people with higher incomes use their superior purchasing power to buy lower density" and "rising incomes and leisure are the basis for a demand for newer houses as such, and in general for more spaciously sited homes."[17] However, upon examining the data he found only a small partial relationship between population density and income.

While the partial coefficient is negative for four of the six cities examined it is significant at the one-tail ten percent level only for one. In view of the strong positive relationship between income and expenditures on housing per household, this can be the case only if the value of housing output per square mile tends to increase with income. The latter relationship is indeed found for all cities examined. Even more puzzling, one finds little partial correlation between income and the proportion of dwellings in single-family structures, which I interpret as varying inversely with the physical output of housing per square mile of land. It would appear that the best explanation for this apparent contradiction is as follows: because of favorable neighborhood effects, the price per unit of housing, and thus land rentals, tends to be greater in higher income areas, offsetting any tendency for higher income households to live at lower population densities but producing a higher value of housing output per unit of land.[18]

Hence, the quality and type of neighborhood are seen to play a large potential role in residential location. The most important explanatory variable that Muth found to explain declining densities was the age of the dwelling unit (i.e., the younger the unit, the lower the density). A possible explanation for this is that people with higher incomes have a preference for newer homes situated on larger and larger plots (as distance from CBD increases), but Muth has already stated the weak relation he found between income and population density, an alternative explanation is that these homes are being occupied by young, growing families that need the more spacious units; but here again Muth has found only a small relation between the two. Therefore, it appears that there is no simple explanation for the density gradient; it is the probable result of many complex factors acting together, which have not yet been successfully accounted for. Muth himself concludes: "Thus, it appears to me that a negative exponential pattern of gross population densities in relation to distance is as good an approximation to actual patterns as any others.[19]

THE LOWRY MODEL

Before examining Lowry's work on Pittsburgh, we shall briefly review the factors that appear to play a significant role in residential location: (1) journey-to-work, (2) family income, (3) size of family, (4) preference function for age of dwelling, (5) occupational type, (6) socioeconomic status, and (7) amenities. Briefly, it is felt by most that factors (3) through (7) are to be included in the "ceteris paribus" assumption when examining the alleged dominance of the journey-to-work relationship (which correctly should include (2) as part of a time–cost function) in determining residential location. Consequently, it will be interesting to examine which of these factors are considered either implicitly or explicitly by Lowry in his empirical examination of residential and retail location in the Pittsburgh area in his work, *Model of a Metropolis.*[20]

The conceptual framework of the Lowry model is not one of economics but rather one of social physics (which has certain economic implications) known as a gravity model. The gravity model predicts that the attraction by a center will be directly proportional to its mass and inversely proportional to the square of distance from it. In Lowry's model, the center is one of basic employment (exogeneous to the model) that exerts a pull on people to live close to it, which in turn creates a market for retail employment center (endogenous) that itself exerts a pull on potential residents and so on until all employment and residential households are located. A complete schematic diagram of the model, which indicates the overall pattern described above in addition to the operational constraints that exist in the model is shown in Figure 3–7.

Lowry states that "the object of this research has been the development of an analytical model capable of assigning urban activities to subareas of a bounded region in accordance with those principles of locational interdependence that could be reduced to quantitative form. The model is not designed to project regional aggregates, such as total employment or population, but rather to allocate such aggregates to locations within the region."[21]

Briefly stated, the model is designed to generate estimates of retail employment, residential population (number of households), and land use for subareas of a bounded region. The estimates are derived from assumptions or from actual data regarding the geographical distribution of basic employment within the region, the amounts a site space occupied by basic establishments and constraints imposed on land use by the physical characteristic of sites by legal restrictions such as gaming laws. Given these inputs, the distributions of residential population and retail employment are generated by means of algebraic functions that relate places of residence to places of work and relate the locations of various types of retail activity to the accessible market of consumers. These functions were developed from an analysis of work- and shopping-trip links based on traffic study data and may be interpreted as roughly expressing the outcome of a competition for sites accessible to the relevant activity. Thus, rather than simulating detailed market processes in which individual establishments (households, business firms, and other activities) compete for sites, the model summarizes these processes by calculating the "potential" of each location as a residential and/or retail site, given the pre-existing distributions of linked activities.[22]

Thus, starting with a given distribution of "basic" workplaces, the computer distributes, around each workplace, a residential population that can supply an appropriate labor force. Since workplaces usually occur in groups, most residential areas thus receive populations that are linked by employment to a number of workplaces. Some areas adjacent to major employment centers are unable to accommodate all the households assigned to them because much of

Figure 3-7. Information Flows in the Pittsburgh Model.

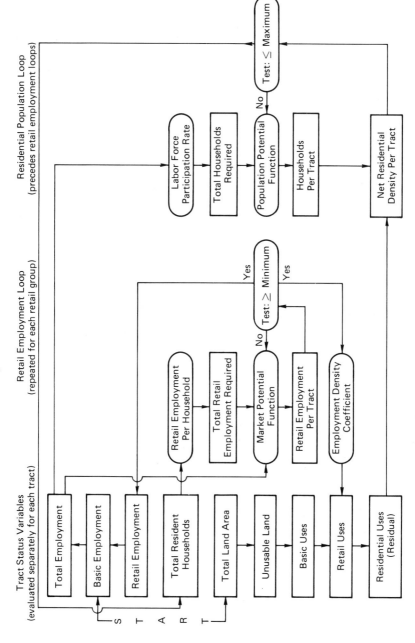

the space has been pre-empted for non-residential uses. The overflow is then reallocated to the remaining proximate areas. This spatially distributed residential population is then available as a base for the location of population-serving activities such as retail and educational facilities. The market potential of each location (in terms of accessible customers) is evaluated; and retail employment is spatially distributed in proportion to these potentials. In a new round of calculations the residences of retail and service employees are located. This event changes the distribution of residential population so that market potentials must be recalculated. Iterations proceed in this manner until a stable co-distribution of all employment and all residences is achieved within the constraints of available land—efficient sales of operation for enterprises and density ceilings for residential population.[23]

It should be noted that the use of this gravity model concept that has just been described was dictated by the type of data that had been collected and by its ease of construction and computation although Lowry himself favors models depicting more of the analytics of rational choice.[24]

Given these severe and realistic problems of data constraints and computational efficiency, let us examine exactly what was produced by the model in terms of its informational output and more importantly the consistency and logic of the output.

In examining the various features of the Lowry model, we will limit the analysis to that of residential location in the model. In order to do this, the model takes into account the multi-nucleated (many employment centers) aspect of most cities, but beyond this most of its workings do not deal with certain other factors that have already been mentioned, due to the lack of data for them or the prohibitive cost of including them. These are (1) although admitting other factors, such as amenities that play an important role in residential location, Lowry's model places its emphasis on the journey-to-work relationship; (2) for an accessibility measure, airline distance alone is used rather than some attempt at a time–cost relationship; (3) it does not include any socioeconomic or occupational characteristics; (4) no price or income factors are included; (5) no differentiation between types of dwelling units; and finally, (6) it takes no account of the time factor in development and generates an "instant" metropolis.[25]

Yet despite these obvious shortcomings, the model does achieve a fairly good fit in allocating residential households with an R^2 of about .62 when regressed against the actual residential distribution of 1958. The implications (and potential criticisms and shortcomings) of this are that the model may be a good predictive device for examining aggregate residential location but does not provide us with any systematic set of parameters that enable us to analyze the mechanics of residential location itself on any reasonable micro level—that is, this model is a macro model whose present function can only be one of aggregate predictions and any attempt to make significant analogies with actual behavior on the micro level are not impossible (as Lowry shows in examining the implications of his density figures) but are nonetheless not very rigorous and perhaps even misleading.[26]

THE LOWRY AND ALONSO MODELS COMPARED

The contrast between the Lowry and Alonso models may now be more striking. The Alonso model is a micro model that ideally (if made to include certain other variables) would replicate the actual locational behavior of households and thus yield structural parameters that were relatively constant and that possessed analytical content or meaning. The problem is that this model or approach has not been empirically tested due to data constraints. The Lowry model, on the other hand, has passed the criterion of empirical testing but again, due to data constraints, was forced to assume a macro form, which produces aggregate predictions and not much real analysis (except by analogy). The model presented in this thesis is basically an attempt at analyzing the micro behavior of households on a theoretical level and also an attempt at empirically verifying the relationships presented with the major emphasis on the implications of the data examined rather than on the theoretical framework itself.

Chapter Four

The Buffalo Model

Before the formal presentation of the statistical model used to analyze residential location in Buffalo, New York, is made, it may prove helpful to examine briefly the objectives of this research, which are threefold: (1) to present a relatively simple theoretical model that analyzes residential location; (2) to examine the data available in a detailed manner in order to test the validity of the model and to point out areas where further research is needed; and (3) to perform simulations with the model to test not only its "goodness of fit" but also the credibility of its workings to see whether such a model can be useful for further research.

The model is a micro-oriented one that locates individual households based on such characteristics as income, size, occupation, race, and so forth. Further, it is basically an economic location model with most of the variables being strictly of the economic type or proxies for economic variables (although there are exceptions). The major constraint affecting the actual variables that were chosen was that of available data. From this data, only those variables that were both meaningful and significant were selected, which resulted in eleven independent variables.

The major portion of the data was obtained from a transportation survey conducted in 1962 by the Niagara Falls Transportation Study.[1] The remaining data came from the 1960 Census of Population for Buffalo.[2]

The data itself is for individual households located in Buffalo proper and a small ring of surrounding suburbs—that is, rings 1 through 3 in Figure 4–1. With the aid of a model, we examined locational behavior of individual households in the greater Buffalo area. Where census data were needed to supplement the traffic study's data, the household locations were determined by using census tract locations (see Figure 4–2), which was provided by the traffic study together with its ring and sector location.

The three rings are further divided into sectors (in Figure 4–1, the

Figure 4–1.   Map of Buffalo—Rings and Sectors.

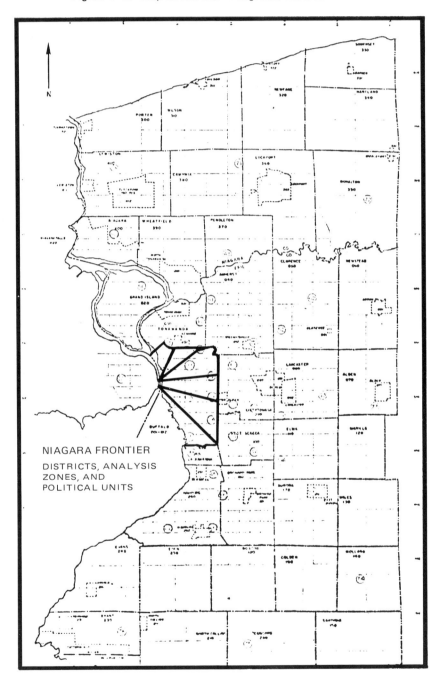

NIAGARA FRONTIER

DISTRICTS, ANALYSIS
ZONES, AND
POLITICAL UNITS

Figure 4–2. Map of Buffalo—Census Tracts.

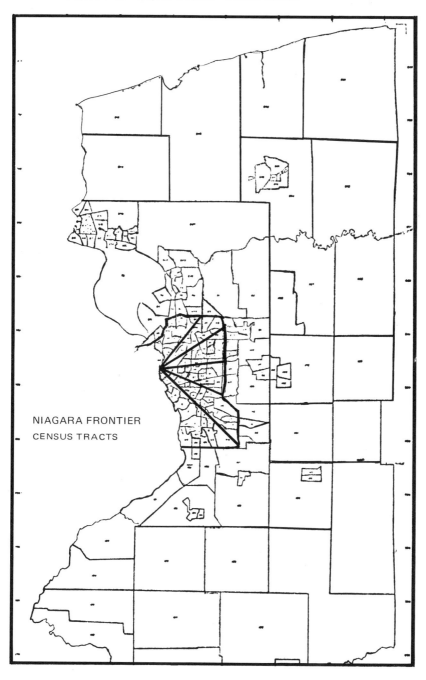

NIAGARA FRONTIER
CENSUS TRACTS

numbers in circles; for example, 20, 21, and so forth) with ring 1 containing four sectors and rings 2 and 3 containing six sectors each. The major movements and allocations predicted and analyzed are those involving movements between rings. Sector (intra-ring) allocations and movements are reflected but not as accurately nor as rigorously.

In its operation, the model attempts to predict and analyze (a) how much households spend on housing per year, (b) where the housing is located, and (c) what type of housing services are consumed.

The functional form of the model can be found in Table 4–1 and the definition of the variables used can be found in Tabel 4–2. All three equations are linear in form and coefficients were estimated using ordinary least squares or two-stage least squares without any logarithmic transformations. The final form of the model using OLS estimators is recursive with the dependent variable from equation (1) becoming an independent variable in equation (2) and the depend-

Table 4–1. Final Functional Form of Buffalo Model

CH = FN (Y, YN, OCCUP)
LOCH = FN (CH, RACE, YN, MODE, ACCTY)
TYPR = FN (CH, LOCH, SZF)
EN DOGENOUS VARIABLES: CH, LOCH, TYPR
EXO GENOUS VARIABLES: Y, YN, OCCUP, MODE, ACCTY, SZF
POLICY VARIABLES: Y, RACE, ACCTY

Table 4–2. Explanation of Variables Used in Buffalo Model

CH	Dollar amount spent per year on housing per household–renters and home owners.
Y	Dollar annual income per household.
YN	Neighborhood median income–based on census tract data–proxy for income class grouping, and so forth.
OCCUP	Refers to occupation–white collar or blue collar–proxy for asset variables based on lifetime earnings–coded (1) for White Collar, (0) for Blue Collar.
LOCH	Refers to location of residence as geographically distant from the central business district–expressed in miles.
RACE	Refers to race–white or non-white.
MODE	Refers to mode of travel used to get to work–auto or rapid transit–coded (1) for auto (0) for rapid transit.
ACCTY	Refers to accessibility to place of work as related to place of residence–is equal to distance of work place from central business district (in miles) times ones income.
TYPR	Refers to type of residence: single family (coded one), two family (coded two), or multifamily (coded three).
SZF	Refers to size of family–by number of members.
PCAR	Refers to number of automobiles owned by the household.
LOCW	Refers to linear distance of head of household's work place from central business distant (CBD).

ent variables from equations (1) and (2) becoming independent variables in equation (3). The recursive nature of the model eliminated the potential problems of simultaneity (discussed at greater length in conjunction with two-stage least squares estimators) and also facilitated the simulations as well as implying a certain decision framework for the residential locator. The rationale for the inclusion of the various independent variables as well as the form of the equations is discussed in conjunction with the empirical results (using OLS) for the Buffalo data.

The final form of the Buffalo model using ordinary least squares to estimate the coefficients can be found in Table 4–3. All of the coefficients were found to be significant at the .001 level except Y in equation (1) and Mode in equation (2), which were significant at the .01 level. The F statistics were all significant at the .01 level by a wide margin which indicates in this case, that the R^2 statistics are highly significant.[3]

In order to partially test for the presence of simultaneous equation bias, the same equations were run using two-stage least squares. The results of this run can be found in Table 4–4. A cursory observation reveals that the two estimating techniques yield almost identical results not only in terms of the actual numerical values of the coefficients but also with regard to the other statistical results presented. The numerical equivalence of the results together with the manner in which the regression algorithms (i.e., OLS + TSLSQ) themselves work indicate that there may not be much, if any, simultaneous equation bias present, which is not too surprising since the use of TSLSQ does yield consistent (but not unbiased) estimates with the bias decreasing as the sample size grows ($N = 570$).[4]

Now that the formal model has been presented and its mode of

Table 4–3. Preliminary Results for Buffalo Model, Ordinary Least Squares

(1)   CH = 318.2965 + .1146Y   + .0091YN + 47.8968 OCCUP
            (24.0673) (.0026)   (.0021)   (14.5190)

Standard Deviation = 167.17 R^2 = .7888 (ADJ)

(2)   LOCH = 1.794 +   .0007 CH   − 1.6373 RACE + .4185 MODE
                (.2771)   (.00018)   (.1970)   (.1857)

            + .0001 YN
              (.0002)

Standard Deviation = 1.4398 R^2 = .2285 (ADJ)

(3)   TYPR = 2.9225 − .0004 CH − .1209 LOCH − .0627 SZF
                (.1114)   (.00008)   (.0178)   (.0163)

Standard Deviation = .6725 R^2 = .1682 (ADJ)

Table 4–4. Preliminary Form of Buffalo Model, Two-Stage Least Squares

---

(1) CH = 318.2965 + .1146 Y + .0091 YN + 47.8968 OCCUP
         (24.0673) (.0026)   (.0028)   (14.5190)

  Standard Deviation = 167.1679 R^2 = .7888

(2) LOCH = 1.8526 + .0007 CH + .0001 YN − 1.6415 RACE
          (.2878)   (.0001)   (.000025)   (.1971)

       + .4347 MODE
         (.1869)

  Standard Deviation = 1.44 R^2 = .2283

(3) TYPR = 2.8295 − .0003 CH − .1242 LOCH − .0651 SZF
           (.1443)   (.00009)   (.0415)   (.0165)

  Standard Deviation = .6734 R^2 = .1659

---

operation indicated, it is necessary to indicate how the various variables were constructed and chosen. In so doing, certain strengths and weaknesses of the model will become apparent both through errors of commission and omission.

SELECTION OF VARIABLES

Equation One

To begin with, the data for the CH variable, which indicates the dollar amount spent per year on housing, was not directly available from the Buffalo traffic data and had to be constructed. For renters (two-family and multi-family dwellings), this was done by taking the family's income level (acquired directly from Buffalo traffic data) and comparing it with the income distribution for that particular census tract, and then attributing its rental level (adjusting for size of family) to approximately the same position on the rental spectrum for that census tract (acquired from census volumes on Buffalo). The rental term used was gross rent, which includes outlays for heat and light in addition to the monthly rental payment.[5] For homeowners, the same methodology of matching relative positions on the income and value of home scale was used.

In order to get a figure for imputed rent from the value of the home, 10 percent of the value of the home was taken to represent imputed rent.[6] Admittedly, both of these methods are quite arbitrary but there are two tests that can be applied to them in order to pass some judgement on their validity. The first and most important (since the main objective was intra-city analysis) was internal consistency—that is, did the rent–income ratio vary widely between the three classes of rental units? The answer to this is that for all three classes, the rent–income ratio was slightly less than .2 (see Table 4–5 for a more detailed analysis). The second criterion is the figure of .2 itself, which also has been found to be a good estimate of the average national rent–income ratio.[7] Further, the fact that our methods yield a figure that is less than .2 can be partially accounted for by the fact that the income statistics are for 1962 whereas the rental and homeowner data is from 1960.

The consumption function or equation states that the amount spent per year on housing is a function of current income, current neighborhood median income, and occupation (all of which were obtained directly from the Buffalo data). In this form the consumption function is really a hybrid of Duesenberry's[8] (YN represents keeping up with the "Joneses") and Modigliani's[9] (occupation is a proxy for the asset role of earnings expectations with white-collar workers having a higher life-time expectancy of earnings than blue-collar workers), which together imply a function with a ratchet effect and one with a permanent income approach, also—that is, it is more than current income that affects household expenditures on housing,[10] it is also one's expectations and realizations (in part) of what one feels will be earned and what one's neighbor is doing with respect to housing. This notion of a "permanent income" type consumption function for housing is certainly not new and has been found to have empirical significance by Reid and Muth among others.[11] In addition, the actual linear results are somewhat similar to what Maisel and Winnick found when they investigated housing expenditures for large cities in the North using the Survey of Consumer Expenditures for 1950 in which their average linear estimate was: CH = 296.30 + .09 Y_G with an R^2 of .66 and where Y_G is gross income.[12]

However, despite an R^2 of .7888, the high significance of the variables and the F-test, and the economically rational approach toward housing expenditures, this equation represents a very simplified attempt to explain housing expenditures and should not be taken as a comprehensive endeavor at explaining this particular phenomenon. Some of the obvious factors (such as size of family and race) that influence housing expenditures appear in the two other equations of the model where it was felt their effect would be either more illuminating or statistically significant. By more illuminating is meant that an attempt has been made to estimate the steps that a consumer makes in determining a residential site, which necessitates the variables appearing in as few equations as possible—that is, the model states that when a consumer goes about the

Table 4–5. Analysis of Rent–Income Ratio for Different Types of Dwelling Units, Buffalo

Rent–Income Ratio	< 1/5	1/5	> 1/5
Single-Family	58%	20%	22%
Two-Family	54%	23%	23%
Multi-Family	55%	25%	20%

process of choosing a potential residential site, the first factor that is examined is his budget constraint. After deciding how much he can afford to spend on housing, he then goes to his preferred area(s) and determines what is being offered there in terms of the rental or purchase price of either an apartment or home. From the spectrum of choices offered, he makes the final choice of what type of dwelling he will reside in. This step-wise action of the model will be further discussed when the actual performance of the model is examined. Certain other factors, such as site amenities were either not available as data inputs or were not statistically significant (see Table 4–6).

A further examination of this equation, using both OLS and TSLSQ indicates that current income (note "t" test) is by far the most important variable influencing current consumption expenditures with YN and OCCUP having approximately equal importance. Certainly the direction of importance is what one would expect but the magnitudes themselves may be open to some criticism. A priori, one would expect a more important role for YN, especially for homeowners. Statistically, this is probably best explained by the relatively low correlation (see Table 4–6) between Y and YN. Also, one's occupation plays a more important empirical role than indicated here,[13] but this is probably due to the rather crude manner in which this variable approximates lifetime expectation of earnings. In summary, the equation for analyzing and predicting consumption expenditures for housing is lacking analytically, which is partially due to the recursive requirements of the model and empirically due to the problems with proxy variables of YN and OCCUP, but nonetheless appears to be a fairly reliable predictor.

Equation Two or LOCH

The second equation attempts to explain the location of the household in terms of linear distance as measured from the Central Business District (see Figures 4–1 and 4–2) or CBD. The functional form of the equation is: LOCH = f_n (CH, RACE, MODE, YN). Briefly, this equation states that the location of the residence is a function of how much is spent on housing, the race of the household, the mode of travel used to get to work (assuming using a car enables one to live farther out than if one is restricted to public transportation), and neighborhood median income (which indicates the tendency for people of the same income class to group together). According to the "t" test, RACE is the most important variable (for both OLS and TSLSQ) in explaining housing location. The sign of this variable is also significant in that it is negative, which indicates that non-whites "ceteris paribus" live closer to the CBD than do whites, which corresponds (based on census data) to the existence of a non-white ghetto in close proximity to the CBD.[14] Therefore, it is the magnitude of the variable that necessitates further explanation. Part of the reason could be that non-whites prefer to spend less on housing than whites of the same income class, and so forth and hence tend to live in those areas where cheaper housing

Table 4–6.   Correlation Matrix for Buffalo Data

	TYPR	SZF	PCAR	Y	YN	CH	AGE	RACE	OCCUP	MODE	LOCH
SZF	-0.19										
PCAR	-0.21	0.13									
Y	-0.20	0.11	0.36								
YN	-0.14	0.05	0.05	0.12							
CH	-0.28	0.13	0.37	0.88	0.17						
AGE	-0.06	-0.29	0.04	0.03	0.03	0.01					
RACE	0.10	0.03	-0.19	-0.13	-0.19	-0.11	-0.05				
OCCUP	0.05	-0.01	0.31	0.23	0.04	0.26	-0.06	-0.24			
MODE	-0.07	0.09	0.40	0.17	-0.04	0.21	-0.13	-0.14	0.19		
LOCH	-0.33	0.08	0.15	0.21	0.28	0.25	-0.06	-0.38	0.12	0.16	
LOCW	-0.06	0.04	0.08	0.03	0.01	0.04	-0.07	-0.03	0.12	0.19	0.13

exists, which are usually located near the CBD. This hypothesis has some statistical evidence to (note blacks only regression run in Chapter Five, Table 5–10) substantiate it.[15] However, this particular empirical result is subject to the rather severe criticism that non-whites spend less because of a housing segregation policy that does not permit them to purchase more housing, and hence it is not clear what the equation is telling us. Therefore, a more reasonable explanation is one of housing segregation by whites against non-whites. The justification for this explanation is that much of the employment in Buffalo is unionized (due to presence of steel and other basic industries), which would tend to produce a rather even income distribution throughout the city (which is substantiated by census data).[16] Therefore, non-whites with equal incomes, family size, and sometimes even consumption expenditures on housing, consistently live closer to the CBD than do whites. Of course, an alternative explanation, which has already been partially breached, is that non-whites simply prefer to live close to the CBD (other than for employment reasons, which will be discussed further on). To my knowledge, there is no research to indicate the latter, but there is ample evidence to indicate the former (i.e., housing segregation).[17] The appearance of YN (second most important factor; Table 4–3) reflects the fact that people of the same income class tend to congregate together. Ideally, the variable would also reflect an ethnic connotation that would undoubtedly enhance the importance of the variable especially in an ethnic town such as Buffalo. In fact, one could hypothesize that in conjunction with CH a ratchet effect could be produced by people remaining, at least initially, in a particular ethnic ghetto due to family and personal ties even though their income, family size, and so forth would dictate their moving into a different neighborhood or area. The inclusion of the CH variable together with its positive sign indicates that as one spends more on housing, there is a tendency, although not a very strong one ($r = .25$), that agrees with Muth's findings for the household to locate further out from the CBD. The final factor that is included is the mode of transportation, either car or public transit, used by the head of the household to get to work. The reasoning here is that the use of a car enhances the mobility of the household and hence enables it to move further out from the main centers of job activity. Of course, an objection could be made that the number of passenger cars owned would be a better variable to use, but this PCAR variable (Table 4–6) has about the same correlation ($r = .15$) with LOCH as does MODE ($r = .16$), but was not significant ($t = 1.8$) when used with other variables in the equation. It is freely admitted that the possession or non-possession of an automobile(s) is a more fundamental variable in that it appears to have a causal effect on location rather than an effect of location, which MODE itself may appear to be. However, it should be remembered that when a family unit is deciding whether to purchase an automobile(s), it is here that the causal factors, which also affect residential location, are taken into account and that once the car(s) is purchased (which the data reflects) all we have is their effect as reflected in the PCAR variable (Table 4–6), just as they are in the MODE variable. Hence, it is felt that both MODE and PCAR reflect the same causes in much the same way, and thus it is their statistical behavior that determines their inclusion or exclusion—that is, the analytical or explanatory role of these two variables in this particular equation is deemed to be about equal and thus the second criterion of statistical significance was employed.

Although the R^2 of this equation of .2285 is by no means high, it is quite good in terms of attempting to explain household behavior on the micro level.[18] Furthermore, all the variables except mode were highly significant and with the correct theoretically implied signs.

Despite this statistical factor, there does appear to be a major flaw in this particular equation, not with respect to what is included, but more importantly because of what is left out. The key variable that is missing is the role of one's workplace in determining one's residential location as a function of distance. Statistically, this exclusion is partially revealed by the fact that the partial correlation coefficient of LOCH and LOCW is only .13, and when LOCW was used in conjunction with any one of the other possible variables to explain LOCH, it was found to be insignificant with t's ranging from 1.5 to .8. This occurs in spite of the enormous significance placed upon it by almost all writers on both a theoretical and empirical level (see Chapter Three).

In order to examine more fully the possible explanations for this result, let us (1) postulate a reason for it; (2) examine how the variable was measured to see whether this is where the flaw lies; (3) try different variables that take the implications or criticisms of (2) into account.

We alluded to a partial explanation in Chapter Three when certain qualifications or variables such as amenities and occupation level were seen to play a rather significant role in residential location. Further, the appearance and significance of both YN and CH in the equation indicate that class clustering and the economic market structure and distribution of potential homesites play an important role in residential location. One could also argue that although families once did locate in accordance with where they worked (in the early days of urban industrial expansion) because there were no autos or good public transit (or they couldn't afford them), they no longer do. This situation has changed in recent years with the increasing importance of the automobile, education, and so forth, such that families now locate where they maximize their locational utility (based on such factors as amenities) in conjunction with their budget constraint and simply commute to work from there (i.e., accessibility to work plays a much smaller role in their locational utility function). A possible test for this hypothesis would be to examine the locational patterns of households in our most rapidly expanding cities such as Los Angeles, Atlanta, and Houston, which when viewed superficially, at least, seem to confirm this notion. Hence, the combined role of such factors as amenities, class clustering, and a changing preference function could dwarf the importance of accessibility.

However, it is not the dwarfing of its role that is indicated here, but rather its almost total insignificance, which phenomenon is quite new and will minimally need the results of (2) and (3) to more fully explain.

The construction of the two variables LOCH and LOCW was very simple, in which the airline distance from the CBD (see Figures 4–1 and 4–2) for home (LOCH) and work (LOCW) were computed and became the data for these variables. When home and work occurred at equal distances (same ring) but not in the same area (sector) such that crosstown commuting was involved, a directional correction took place, which was added on to LOCW. For example, if the household were located in ring 1, sector 1 and the workplace was located in ring 1, sector 3, the distance from the CBD is the same, which does not take into account the crosstown element of commuting that does take place. So one-half of this distance was added on to LOCW to reflect this. However, by only taking half of this distance, a bias in favor of LOCW is introduced; and so, despite even this bias, the result of an r of .13 was achieved.

In determining LOCW though, only the head of the household's workplace was considered. Of course, this is a serious omission in that many households do have two members working; and it seems reasonable that some trade-off would be made in order to move toward maximizing joint accessibility. This only establishes an error in direction but not magnitude. The issue is whether it is really one of such magnitude so as to distort the findings as much as they appear to be—that is, only about 38 percent of the households reporting had more than one member working, and of these, 55 percent of the secondary members worked in the same sector or no more than one sector from their homes, which tends to confirm the hypothesis that secondary household workers are usually part-time workers who seek employment close to home. Although this is not a very definitive or rigorous examination of this particular omission (and is not intended to be so), it does indicate that this is probably not where the major distortion has occurred.

The use of airline distance from CBD as a measure of accessibility is the concept most susceptible to criticism as we saw from Chapter Three. This is particularly true from an economic viewpoint where the variable really should be a time–cost one in which time– (rather than distance) cost is function of income. Why, then, was airline distance used? In order to best answer this question, we will begin by asserting that the most desirable variable would probably be a combination of income and travel time since it is a simple concept and yields a time–cost relationship. Therefore, the first task to be explained is why distance was substituted for time in equation (2).

The answer to this is both pragmatic and empirical. From an empirical standpoint, Keefer (for Pittsburgh), Pendleton (for Washington, D.C.), and Mills (for Chicago, Detroit, et al.) found the correlation between time and airline distance to be in the neighborhood of $R^2 = .92$.[19] From a more pragmatic viewpoint, if one is to use time rather than distance as a variable in an accessibility function, it becomes necessary to separate out only that portion of time that is used in actual travel when using similar modes (i.e., time getting to and from one's car should be subtracted out for car users). However, when the modes are different, such as car and bus, then the entire commuting time becomes important. In addition to these considerations, the time of day at which the trip occurs is quite relevant since movement at rush hour periods usually varies greatly with non-rush hour movements, especially with regard to freeway travel. In this regard, it is interesting to note that Pendleton, Mills, and Keefers' findings apply equally well to rush hour periods. In short, the use of airline distance from the CBD appears to be not only simpler but almost as accurate as using time as a measure of accessibility.

The next exercise was to determine whether some simple combination of distance (time) and income could be found that reflects time–cost and is statistically significant. Consider two possibilities: (1) a ratio of income divided by distance, which yields a cost per mile index (as income rises, so does cost per mile, which is a desirable prediction; however, as distance rises, cost falls, which is perverse but this perversion may be swamped by income rising proportionately faster than distance); and (2) a simple multiplicative function of income times distance, which tends to rise with rises in distance and income. Although the second alternative is somewhat more appealing in that it contains no contradictions, it is not necessarily the best approach so natural logs were run in a regression using both income and distance to explain LOCH. The results indicate that the second approach (i.e., the regression coefficients were both positive and less than 1) was the more desirable one. Table 4–7 shows the coefficients of the new LOCH multiple regression equation when accessibility is added to it. In this context, it does reveal a statistically significant role for work accessibility but magnitudinally not a very important one, which is in accordance with the previous discussion of accessibility.

Furthermore, a glance at the correlation matrix (Table 4–8) for the new system of variables including ACCTY (accessibility) seems to indicate that it is income and not distance (i.e., r between Y and LOCH is .21 and between LOCW and LOCH is .13) that plays the major role in accessibility considerations.

Table 4–7. Amended LOCH Analysis to Include Accessibility Variable

LOCH = 1.879 + .0006 CH + .0001 YN − 1.6278 RACE + .3668 MODE
(.2790) (.00018) (.000024) (.1963) (.1863)

+ .0059 ACCTY
(.0025)

where ACCTY = (LOCW * Y) /1000

Standard Deviation + 1.434 R^2 = .2346

Table 4–8. Correlation Matrix for Buffalo Data, Plus Accessibility Variable

	TYPR	SZF	PCAR	Y	YN	CH	AGE	RACE	OCCUP	MODE	LOCH	LOCW
SZF	-0.2											
PCAR	-0.21	0.13										
Y	-0.20	0.11	0.36									
YN	-0.14	0.05	0.05	0.12								
CH	-0.28	0.13	0.37	0.88	0.17							
AGE	-0.06	-0.28	-0.04	0.03	-0.03	-0.01						
RACE	0.10	0.03	-0.19	-0.13	-0.19	-0.11	-0.05					
OCCUP	-0.05	-0.01	0.31	0.23	0.04	0.26	-0.06	-0.24				
MODE	-0.07	0.10	0.40	0.17	-0.04	0.21	-0.13	-0.14	0.19			
LOCH	-0.33	0.08	0.15	0.21	0.28	0.25	-0.06	-0.38	0.12	0.16		
LOCW	-0.07	0.04	0.08	0.03	0.01	0.04	-0.07	-0.03	0.12	0.19	0.13	
ACCTY	-0.14	0.05	0.21	0.50	0.06	0.45	-0.02	-0.08	0.18	0.20	0.20	0.81

ACCTY = Y = LOCW

This agrees with Kain's finding that richer people use more expensive commuting methods in order to save on time. Its relationship to YN also seems to confirm the residential location patterns of cities such as Los Angeles in which the rich are dispersed by neighborhoods (YN role) with these dispersions not being as close as possible to the CBD, but also are not on the fringes of the city (role of accessibility). Of course, this assumes many of these people do work in the CBD, which is not an unreasonable assumption since this is usually the financial and trade center of a municipal area and hence is where many of the higher paying jobs are located. In short, accessibility is statistically significant but more importantly its magnitudinal importance remains relatively minor.

Equation Three

The third equation analyzes the type of dwelling rented or owned by the household. The data was coded one for single-family dwellings, two for two-family dwellings, and three for multi-family dwellings. Hence, the negative signs on the coefficients indicate that as that particular variable rises in value, the household approaches living in a single-family dwelling. A definite conceptual problem arose in treating two-family dwelling units and their respective households as either renters or homeowners, since it is often the case that such dwellings are co-owned or at least one of the two parties owns it all.[20] Nonetheless, it was decided to treat them as renters, which eventually was vindicated in that the rent–income ratios for these households and single-family units was almost identical (see Table 4–5).

The task now becomes one of analyzing the implications of equation three. LOCH is the most significant variable in explaining variations in TYPR, which implies that as one moves out farther and farther from the CBD, the more likely is it that one will live in a single-family unit. This says much more about the economic landscape facing the consumer than it does about the residential locational decision process itself. In fact, it could be argued that the order of equations (2) and (3) should be reversed so that TYPR could appear as an independent variable with more explanatory value in analyzing LOCH rather than having LOCH play mainly a predictive role in equation (3), but this was not done because the net R^2 of equations (2) and (3) is better served by the present approach.

The CH variable states that as one spends more on housing, in absolute terms, the type of housing consumed will be that of a single-family unit—that is, as a family moves from an apartment to its own home, this usually involves an upgrading of the housing services consumed (particularly in terms of density), which necessitates a higher expenditure. A further implication of this variable and the way it enters into the equation is that families will normally upgrade their housing by a move to either a better home or from an apartment to a home rather than from a home to a luxury apartment. However, if one postulates that the move from a home to a luxury apartment is accompanied by a decrease in family size with no appreciable decline in housing expenditures or perhaps even a small decline (e.g., movement by some couples from suburbs to luxury apartments nearer the CBD as their children move away from home), then the equation is accurate in its analysis. The equation breaks down most dramatically in failing to predict the movement of households (probably young families), which simultaneously increase their housing expenditures by moving from one apartment to a better or larger apartment, and their family size, such that density is not reduced. Of course, it could be argued that this in itself is only an intermediate step toward their eventual goal of homeownership, which again leaves the equation intact. As has already been alluded to, the SZF variable predicts that as family size increases "ceteris paribus" the type of unit desired moves to a lower density level (e.g., a family moves from an apartment to a two-family unit to a single-family unit). This predicted sequence, vis-à-vis family size, has substantial empirical validity.[21]

Unfortunately, neither of the variables themselves (r of $-.33$ for LOCH, r of $-.28$ for CH, and r of $-.19$ for SZF) nor in linear combination (R^2 of .1682) tell us very much about why households desire one type of unit rather than another, which is probably the result of the following: (1) the analysis being on a micro level; (2) the choice of basically economic and social variables, which are often inadequate to explain such complex phenomenon as housing choice; and (3) the equation being linear in form. More gratifying is the fact that the variables do have the correct signs, that their inclusion does make sense and can be justified, and finally that the workings of the equation itself appears to yield valid predictions.

A CRITIQUE OF THE MODEL

Before turning to the model's simulation performance, a brief discussion of some of its potential major shortcomings is appropriate. These are (1) no price variable is included in any of the equations; (2) no site or area amenities are included; (3) the model is too simplified for what it is trying to explain; (4) the relatively high standard deviations may lead to wide confidence intervals for the dependent variables.

First Criticism: No Price Variable

There are really two answers to the first criticism, which again are pragmatic and theoretical. From a pragmatic viewpoint, the requisite data on prices were not available and the problems associated with going to Buffalo and deriving them based on 1962 conditions was deemed prohibitive. The theoretical reply is a much more involved one. To begin with, prices could probably (if available) appear in equations (1), (2) or (3) or all of them. However, in actual fact CH is really an implicit price of housing variable and does appear in equations (2) and (3) as an independent variable. Thus, the absence of an actual price variable is most crucial in equation (1). Here it was felt that what was needed was not a crosssection series of prices but rather a time series of prices in order to better analyze how consumers reacted to changes in the relative prices of various types of housing. In this way, both the substitution and income affects with regard to housing could be examined. This data being unavailable, it was decided to use what really amounts to an income-consumption curve (Engle curve) for housing, which is viewed as being more stable between income and housing classes, and thus more valid for use with simulations.

Britton Harris has also emphasized the need for relative prices:

> If values (prices) are made explanatory variables leading to changes in the behavior of decision units, then future applications of the same theory and its derivative models require that these values be projected under new circumstances. The theorist then faces an ugly dilemma. If he chooses to predict future prices by means of proxy variables, he must build a purely descriptive model for this purpose, which contains no ideas about cause and effect; and this being the case, he might just as well have left prices out of the original analysis and included the same proxy variables, admitting from the outset that his theory was in part purely descriptive. If on the other hand, he takes the importance of these economic variables seriously, he must face the difficulty of reconstructing a complete market through some form of simulation. This reconstruction is complicated by the existence of submarkets, institutional stickiness, imperfect dissemination of information and probable lags in equilibrium.[22]

Second Criticism: No Amenities

Amenities such as quality of schools, garbage collection, and so forth, did not appear because they were not available from the original data. Furthermore, it does not seem possible that they could have been obtained even by going to the desired resident sites in Buffalo (which has already been deemed prohibitive)—that is, the data that is required is the perception (as distinct from objective existence) and relative importance of the particular amenity by the site occupant when the site was occupied for the study. This is basically a subjective approach because the occupant may have only been aware of some of the neighborhood amenities and each occupant may have a preference pattern for them which departs drastically from that of his neighbors. Unfortunately, it is exactly this type of amenity (i.e., quality of schools) that may play a very dominant role in residential location, but this cannot be determined until better data is collected.

The Buffalo model, though, is not completely void of amenity variables as both RACE and YN, which appear in equation two, can be viewed as a type of amenity that involves living with people whose characteristics are most amenable. In fact, one empirical investigation of certain amenities in Raliegh, North Carolina, indicated a significant role for class type variables.[23]

The crucial question with regard to amenities vis-à-vis the Buffalo model is whether their inclusion would reinforce or negate its analysis and predictions. Although one cannot say much conclusively without actual data, certain assertions can be made with some degree of certitude. They would not enter in equation (1), so this one can be eliminated from discussion. Equation (2) already has two amentiy variables included. Others that might be included are quality of schools, street lighting, level of crime, and so forth. One can assert that these types of amenities are usually found to be better at greater distances from the CBD (more true of schools than lighting), which would mean that their inclusion would yield positive coefficients and a higher total R^2 for the equation. A further effect would be to change the relative importance and effects of all variables yielding a more reliable (assuming the variables were found to be significant) and reasonable prediction of household location. The key point here is that the inclusion of more amenity variables would not alter the equation in such a way as to produce results that directly refute present predictions. To be more specific, it would not change the directions indicated by any variable nor would it so change its relative magnitude as to make it meaningless with the possible exception of YN, which might have to be reformulated to more accurately reflect its class implications (e.g., a percent of ratio).

With equation (3), the problem becomes somewhat more complex as it is easy to conceive of a trade-off taking place between amenities and TYPR (as it was with amenities and LOCH). The problem then becomes an empirical one of determining what type of dwellings are usually accompanied by the highest level of amenities. Again, at the risk of great oversimplification, the answer appears to be single-family homes although this situation is rapidly changing such that for certain areas the inclusion of amenities in equation (3) would produce a small positive coefficient. For this study, it would probably produce a somewhat larger (in absolute value) negative coefficient.

In short, the inclusion of amenities would not alter the predictions of the model but would, in general, increase their sophistication and explanatory value. The major reason is that amenities are usually associated with higher rental (implicit or explicit) values that occur most often in the outlying areas of our residential economic plain. Hence, their inclusion would produce coefficients with signs that enforce rather than negate present predictions.

Third Criticism: Model Too Simple

On a purely theoretical level, there is certainly much validity to the third criticism. Residential location is indeed a very complex phenomenon in which economic, sociological, psychological, and political variables all play a significant role. Even though the emphasis in this study is on economic variables and their proxies, even here the analysis seems grossly simplified (e.g., presence of few amenities as discussed previously). Further, this particular model is demand oriented, and since the unit of analysis is the household, it is also a micro model. Thus, to enhance its operation and usefulness, a supply constraint was introduced.

The supply constraint is more macro oriented and provides linear aggregate constraints to the operation of the micro model. More explicitly, the supply constraints operate as upper bounds on allocating the number of households locating in a particular sector. For example, if the demand side of the model allocates 50 single-family residential locators to ring 1, sector 1, this amount of single-family residences is compared with the supply of single-family residences for ring 1, sector 1, as yielded by the supply function. If the demanded amount exceeds the supply constraint, the excess is allocated outward (i.e., ring 2, sector 1) if the household is white, but kept stationery if the household is non-white. No price adjustment is attempted, which makes the model adjustment descriptive rather than analytic in its operation.

Since the supply function or constraint has not been discussed yet, it may prove helpful to digress on it. The constraint is a simple linear function consisting of density, employment, and zoning variables as independent variables. These were chosen for both their explanatory value and statistical significance. In constructing the function, there were five variables, for which data were readily available, that might be useful in explaining the supply of housing of a particular type in a particular sector or zone of the city. These were (1) zoning laws (ZOLAW and ZOLWR), (2) sector employment (ZOEMP), (3) geographical area (AREA), (4) distance from the central business district (CBDT), and (5) accessibility to and from the sector (ACCES). The statistical interrelationships between these five are illustrated in the correlation matrix found in Table 4—9 with a definition of each variable in Table 4—10. It is obvious both on statistical and theoretical grounds that even these few variables are actually examining the same phenomenon—that is, for most cities, as one moves out from the CBD, accessibility declines rather dramatically to the extent that CBDT and ACCES are actually measuring the same phenomenon. Of course, where this is not so true (e.g., Oklahoma City) both variables could be employed. Further, the partial correlation coefficient between the two, which indicates their statistical correlation is .88, implies serious potential multi-collinearity problems if they are both used as independent variables. Similarly, area and density of population (i.e., population/area) explain almost the same phenomenon with density being chosen because it is a sector's density and not just its geographical area that will dictate, through land prices and other factors, what type of housing will be available. With a partial correlation coefficient of −.54 between DEN and AREA, multi-collinearity could affect the coefficients in a perverse manner (depending on whether .54 exceeds the partial correlation coefficient between either area or density and the dependent variable). Zonal or sector employment and zoning law are not interrelated in the way that previous variables are, which leads to a regression containing accessibility, density, employment and zoning constraints. However, when regressions were run using

Table 4–9.   Correlation Matrix for Supply Function, Buffalo

	SH1	SH2	SH3	ZOLAW	ZOEMP	AREA	CBDT	ACCES	ZOLWR
SH2	0.49								
SH3	0.33	0.54							
ZOLAW	0.57	0.04	0.08						
ZOEMP	0.59	0.70	0.25	0.25					
AREA	0.50	-0.11	-0.37	0.38	0.46				
CBDT	0.50	-0.26	-0.43	0.57	0.14	0.87			
ACCES	-0.38	0.33	0.43	-0.36	-0.04	-0.78	-0.88		
ZOLWR	0.31	-0.18	-0.31	0.79	-0.09	0.26	0.55	-0.33	
DEN	0.17	0.67	0.71	0.14	0.39	-0.54	-0.63	0.67	-0.12

Table 4–10. Definition of Variables Used in Supply Function

SH1	Supply of single-family residences on a per sector basis.
SH2	Supply of two-family residences on a per sector basis.
SH3	Supply of multi-family residences on a per sector basis.
ZOLAW	Zoning for the sector coded low for industrial and commercial; high for residential total.
ZOEMP	Total employment for the sector.
AREA	Geographical area of the sector in square miles.
CBDT	Linear average distance of the sector from the central business district.
ACCES	Accessibility to and from the sector coded higher for greater accessibility.
ZOLWR	Alternative zone coding for each sector with more Skewness than ZOLAW.
DEN	Density of population per square mile of area.

these four variables, almost none of them came out significantly, and in addition, the signs of the coefficients were perverse due to multi-collinearity, which necessitated reducing the analysis to three independent variables. The question then became one of what three variables should be chosen. The trade-off was one between explanatory value and inter-dependence with other variables.

Probably the most important exogenous variable to the urban system, which also turns out to be the most statistically independent of the remaining three variables, is ZOEMP. The choice of the remaining two variables was not quite as simple or elegant. A cursory view of Table 4–9 indicates the choice should be between the selection of either ACCES or DEN because of the relative high correlation coefficient of .67 between them and further because it is alleged that the higher the accessibility the higher will be the density. However, this study is indirectly questioning that very hypothesis by claiming that other factors significantly effect density levels. Hence, DEN and ACCES together with ZOEMP were run together and produced the results shown in Table 4–11. Certainly, there is nothing spectacular about them except that DEN fares better than ACCES. In equation (1), the positive signs on ZOEMP and DEN are the opposite of what one would expect (i.e., as employment and density rose the supply of single-family structures should decline). As for ZOEMP, this is partially explained by the data (see Table 4–12) in that high levels of employment are recorded in sectors 1, 2, and 3 of ring 3.[24] The behavior of the DEN coefficient can be explained in part by its high correlation (r of .67) with ACCES. In equation (2), all the coefficient's positive signs appear to be correct but here the multi-collinearity may well have affected the standard errors, and thus "t"-tests of the coefficients for ACCES and DEN in that Table 4–9 implies that DEN should have been significant (i.e., r of .67 between DEN and SH2). Finally, equation (3) contains what first appears to be perverse negative signs on ZOEMP and ACCES. These negative signs can be explained, though, if a sector is

Table 4–11. Preliminary Regression Results for Supply Functions, OLS, Buffalo

(1) SH1 = 21.2084 + .2307 ZOEMP + .3988 DEN – 4.7730 ACCES
       (5.7208)   (.1423)   (.2394)   (1.884)

   Standard Deviation = 4.6109 R^2 = .4728

(2) SH2 = – 3.6681 + .6046 ZOEMP + .5507 DEN + .9571 ACCES
       (8.6242)   (.2144)   (.3608)   (2.8407)

   Standard Deviation = 6.9511 R^2 = .6061

(3) SH3 = 1.5829 – .0620 ZOEMP + .8922 DEN – 1.1284 ACCES
                                                    (2.8496)

   Standard Deviation = 6.9729 R^2 = .3808

zoned such that manufacturing employment can occur in the same sector where multiple unit housing structures exist. Hence, as employment rises, which could imply an increasing area occupied by manufacturing, the supply of multiple unit housing would decline, which would yield a negative sign in the multiple correlation. By the same reasoning, a negative sign for ACCES would also be produced. At the risk of being too repetitive, the same result could be produced by multicollinearity between ACCES and DEN via the ACCES variable (i.e., r between DEN and ACCES is .69 whereas r between ACCES and SH3 is .43).

Due to at least the potentially serious multi-collinearity problems present when ACCES and DEN are used together, the variable ZOLWR was substituted for ACCES and run together with ZOEMP and DEN (see Table 4–13). This variable, ZOLWR, refers to how a sector is zoned with higher coded data being related to the more restricted areas (e.g., residential housing only). Of course, the exact effect of zoning restrictions, is very difficult to determine as zoning laws often change "ex post" (i.e., to rationalize what already has occurred, rather than playing a strictly causal role as is often assumed). Nonetheless, its inclusion did yield reasonable results in terms of directions predicted (i.e., signs of coefficients) for itself and the other variables that appeared with it. This is at least partially due to the elimination of multicollinearity problems with the possible exception of the ZOEMP variable in equation (1) (i.e., r between ZOEMP and DEN is .39 whereas r between DEN and SH1 is .17), which was not related to the inclusion of ZOLWR. However, it should be noted that the substitution of ZOLWR for DEN did not affect either the R^2 or the number of significant variables to any great degree, which indicates that the problem in this general area is due to an attempt to explain a very complex phenomenon with too few variables and too few observations. Rather than trimming the equations any further, though, to include only significant variables, it was decided to leave them in their present state since the supply

Table 4–12. Data for Supply Functions, Buffalo

RING	SECTOR	SH1	SH2	SH3	ZOLAW	ZOEMP	AREA	CBDT	ACCES	ZOLWR	DEN
1	1	25.00	37.00	37.00	5.80	21.80	1.80	2.20	4.00	2.80	27.80
1	2	10.00	14.00	5.00	5.70	12.20	1.40	1.80	4.00	3.80	24.60
1	3	8.00	18.00	19.00	5.90	18.70	2.50	1.50	5.00	2.90	24.50
1	4	5.00	5.00	5.00	2.00	2.30	1.60	1.60	4.00	1.70	4.80
2	1	11.00	9.00	6.00	5.30	13.90	2.70	3.00	4.00	3.60	14.60
2	2	7.00	14.00	3.00	6.00	13.10	3.00	3.30	4.00	4.00	10.80
2	3	18.00	37.00	3.00	5.00	20.10	3.00	3.40	4.00	3.50	17.60
2	4	15.00	32.00	10.00	4.00	35.60	6.20	3.30	4.00	2.80	14.90
2	5	12.00	17.00	3.00	4.80	13.00	4.50	3.50	3.00	3.30	7.10
2	6	5.00	5.00	3.00	3.00	7.10	5.00	3.40	3.00	2.30	3.90
3	1	12.00	17.00	5.00	6.00	18.60	6.30	5.40	2.00	3.30	7.50
3	2	26.00	23.00	4.00	6.50	41.00	10.00	5.80	2.00	3.20	11.40
3	3	17.00	11.00	6.00	6.50	17.30	6.30	5.70	3.00	3.40	3.60
3	4	18.00	5.00	3.00	6.50	8.60	6.80	5.70	3.00	4.40	3.40
3	5	17.00	5.00	3.00	6.50	6.40	6.00	5.90	2.00	4.50	3.00
3	6	17.00	7.00	4.00	6.50	13.50	6.30	5.80	2.00	3.80	5.80

constraints are not functionally related to the demand aspect of the model and have been relegated to a very minor role of serving as an upper bound on settlement based on a simple linear relation in order to add a bit of reality and sophistication to the overall analysis.

Fourth Criticism: High Standard Deviations

The fourth and final general criticism may well be the most important particularly if the model were to be used in conjunction with policy changes or for predictive purposes or a combination of these purposes. With regard to the final demand model, the confidence limits of the respective dependent variables at the .05 level are found in Table 4–14.

It should be obvious that when examined more carefully the fourth objection is invalid because the confidence limits are not very wide which statis-

Table 4–13. Final Regression Results, Supply Functions, OLS, Buffalo

(1) SH1 $= -$ 2.895 $+$ .3998 ZOEMP $-$ .0228 DEN $+$ 3.1599 ZOLWR
            (6.9637)   (.1419)   (0.1779)   (1.8227)

Standard Deviation = 5.1082 R^2 = .3530

(2) SH2 $=$ 3.0165 $+$ .5687 ZOEMP $+$ .6304 DEN $-$ 1.1618 ZOLWR
            (9.434)   (.1924)   (.2411)   (2.4694)

Standard Deviation = 6.9203 R^2 = .6877

(3) SH3 $=$ 8.0358 $-$ .0350 ZOEMP $+$ .7601 DEN $-$ 2.7204 ZOLWR
            (9.0852)   (.1852)   (.2322)   (2.3781)

Standard Deviation = 6.6643 R^2 = .4344

Table 4–14. One-Sided Confidence Intervals for the Three Dependent Variables of the Buffalo Model

CH $=$ 1147.66 $\pm$ 14.0
LOCH $=$ 3.64 $\pm$ .12
TYPR $=$ 1.8 $\pm$ .055

Formula: Confidence limits $= x \pm Z \propto \dfrac{\partial}{\sqrt{N}}$

where $\bar{x}$ = mean

Z = value of t or normal distribution at given of confidence x

∂ = standard deviation

N = sample size

Source: Samuel Richmond, *Statistical Analysis* (Ronald Press, New York, 1964), pp. 162–3.

tically is due to the relationship between the standard deviation and the size of the sample. At the risk of being too presumptuous, it appears that none of the four objections is, as yet, crucial to the operation of the model, so let us proceed on to its actual performance where one or more or perhaps some new short-coming of the model will become apparent.

DIGRESSION ON THE WORKINGS
OF THE BUFFALO MODEL

However, before examining the dynamics of the demand model, a brief digression may be helpful in illuminating exactly what the model is and is not telling us. Basically the model attempts to predict and analyze how much a particular household will spend on housing per year (based on Y, YN and OCCUP), how this budget constraint together with RACE, MODE and YN, and ACCTY predict location, and finally, how CH, LOCH and SZF influence the type of dwelling rented or TYPR. The actual choice process is a very interdependent one with the independent variables having feedback effects on themselves (e.g., the size of one's family affects CH, LOCH and TYPR as well as MODE and YN, but in the model these variables are relegated to where they play the most important role). As mentioned previously, the model is not fixed into its present format, which may not even be the best possible order or form for the variables to appear in order to yield the maximum amount of analysis and prediction. The particular format was chosen for its simplicity, logic, and analytical value and awaits its performance test. It is admittedly a simplistic analysis of a complex phenomenon, but nonetheless, this analysis hopes to isolate and shed greater light on some of the major factors that influence residential locational decisions. It appears to be sufficient for this task.

At this point, the major failure of the model is the low level of importance attached to the location of one's workplace vis-à-vis one's home. Consequently, the traditional economic view of residential location that was conceived as basically a trade-off between site rent and transport costs (of the head of the household) is very much weakened. The reason is that what was originally held constant (e.g., amenities) now distorts the simple trade-off so much that it alone will yield incorrect predictions. In functional form, residential location can be seen as follows: Res Loc $= F_n$ (SITE RENT, TRANSPORT COSTS, INCOME, CLASS, SITE, AMENITIES, RACE, and so forth). The first formulations of the problem held everything in the parentheses except site rent and transport costs constant and dealt with the trade-off between these two. This model does not deny the validity of this approach or the trade-off implied. It merely seeks to enlarge the area of trade-off to include more variables and to determine the relative importance of them. In fact, it is entirely possible and valid to include amenities or even race in the site rent variable—that is, as the ghetto expands in a dynamic urban area, the site rents on land change, which reflects the forces of supply and demand changes that in turn affect residential location. This enlarged trade-off area is one way to explain the results of the model.

Another explanation for the traditional approach and its breakdown is an historical one that incorporates the changing nature of urban structure and technology—that is, one can imagine a dynamic situation in which both views of residential location are valid, but with this particular Buffalo model being the more modern one. In the past, workers probably did originally live close to where they worked, particularly in manufacturing and certain retail establishments of an ethnic nature for the following reasons:

1. Rapid transit was not extensive and was inefficient; and with no automobiles or few available or attainable, it became mandatory to live close to work.
2. Land surrounding certain manufacturing areas was basically undesirable due to smog, dirt, noise, and so forth, which created low land values per capita, which had strong appeal for low-wage (immigrant) labor.
3. Immigrant groups tended to band together into ethnic neighborhoods for political and economic reasons.
4. Certain retail establishments were set up to serve the needs of a particular group.
5. Basic manufacturing employment and retail employment of an ethnic nature formed a much higher percentage of the labor force than they presently do due to increase in services, and so forth.

For these reasons there was a high correlation between the location of one's place of employment and one's home. It would be interesting to investigate the locational behavior of the higher income groups of this period (e.g., managers, bankers, doctors, and others) to determine the extent to which their residential location was also tied to employment location.

However, as time passed, certain events occurred that helped destroy or eliminate the strong bond between residence and workplace:

1. As income rose, people sought new surroundings, which often resulted in more ethnically heterogeneous neighborhoods, but these were still bound by economic constraints. Also, rising incomes did not necessarily mean a change of employment (e.g., steel) in that a worker would continue to commute to the same workplace from his new residential location.
2. As the old workers left their homes, new residents (usually black) moved into their homes. Since they were often much poorer, they increased the density of the occupied dwellings—that is, the low land values necessitated that any new immigrants, who were also poor, must locate in the areas near the original poor immigrants. However, when certain of these new people were able to raise their incomes enough to move (which was difficult due to

racial segregation in employment and education), they were prevented from moving out due to housing segregation.

3. Government subsidies in the form of FHA loans encouraged the move into single-family dwellings by middle-income families, who often were second- and third-generation families, which because of space requirements, spread the city out residentially without a commensurate spreading out of employment centers.

4. The advent of mass ownership of the automobile enabled people to commute farther in the same amount of time (at least in the beginning), which further enforced the first three events.

5. More than one worker in the family forced locational compromises.

6. Families became more interested in neighborhood advantages and disadvantages such as quality of schools, rather than just employment accessibility.

The combination of and increasing importance of these factors has led to the creation of a more complex residential location function in which the trade-off has become one between site rent, race, amenities, and so forth, rather than one between site rent and transport costs for the head of the household.

Of course, the diminished importance given to employment location may be due to the elementary fault of not representing accessibility accurately. This is freely admitted, but this factor alone should not obscure the importance of those factors already enumerated.

Chapter Five

Dynamic Workings
of the Buffalo Model

INTRODUCTION

This chapter presents the dynamic workings of the Buffalo model by examining
the results of four separate simulation experiments. These four experiments
analyze both policy variables and certain mechanical relations that test the
model's ability to produce meaningful predictions when it is "shocked" in
various ways.

FOUR SIMULATIONS

First Simulation

The first simulation is a very simple one in which the data are run
through the regression model with the resultant allocation of households by
location and housing type. These simulation results are then compared with the
actual allocation of households by location and housing type. This indicates the
model's ability to analyze, in a more dynamic context, how the different
independent and dependent variables in the model interact to allocate households within the city. In addition, it plays a predictive role in indicating certain
changes in density and housing type inhabited that may occur in the future
development of the city. Certain weaknesses of the regression model are
examined and discussed, particularly with regard to prediction.

Second Simulation

The second simulation is a policy-oriented one that examines two
possible strategies to break up the ghetto. One possible strategy or policy would
be to increase blacks' income, which would enable them to more effectively bid
for available housing throughout the city. This policy reflects the views of those
who feel that the existence of the ghetto is due more to economic factors

associated with insufficient income than to such factors as segregation, and so forth. To reflect this view, the income of all black families was increased by $1,000, which produced changes in location and housing type inhabited.

The second strategy or policy reflects the opposite viewpoint that the ghetto is largely a result of a segregationist housing policy on the part of white urban residents. The solution in this case is seen to be the vigorous enforcement of a stringent open-occupancy law. This policy was simulated by reducing the negative coefficient on the RACE variable to 0, which implies completely effective open occupancy.

The results of these two opposite strategies are then compared for their effectiveness and their implications for the housing market.

Simulation Three: Technical Change

The third simulation attempts to deal with the problems of urban sprawl and/or congestion as related to accessibility. Simply put, the simulation analyzes the change produced by increasing accessibility to work for those employed in ring 1 of the model (i.e., center city). This is done through the model by reducing the distance (time) component of the accessibility variable (accessibility equals income times distance) by one-half for those employed in ring 1. The increase in accessibility could either increase urban sprawl or produce an increase in employment density for ring 1 or both. The model indicates which of these alternatives (or some other) seems most likely. This simulation also reveals some glaring weaknesses of the model and its applications.

Simulation Four: An Allocation
Comparison

This simulation compares the allocation results from using a regression model based only on data from rings 1 and 2 (city only) versus the allocation results based on a regression model using data only from ring 3 (suburb only)—that is, it examines the differences in locational preferences of city residents versus suburban residents to determine whether suburban residents are simply city residents with more money. In other words, are suburban residents' location preferences only a logical or obvious extension of the location preferences of city residents?

This then is a brief outline of the simulations presented in this chapter. The next task is the analysis of these simulations.

MECHANICAL CONSTRUCTION
OF THE SIMULATIONS

Mechanically, the first simulation was performed by running the entire set of data through the recursive model shown in Table 5–1, which is the final form of the Buffalo model (using OLS). The results for LOCH and TYPR as yielded by

Table 5-1. Buffalo Regression Equations, Ordinary Least Squares

(1) CH = 318.2539 + .1146 Y .0091 YN + 48.1938 OCCUP
       (24.0803) (.0026) (.0028)   (14.5263)

Standard Deviation = 167.2499 R^2 = .7887

(2) LOCH = 1.8790 + .00055 CH + .00013 YN − 1.6279 RACE
       (.2790) (.00018)   (.000021)   (.19632)

       + .3669 MODE + .0058 ACCTY
         (.1863)   (.00247)

Standard Deviation = 1.4341 R^2 = .2346

(3) TYPR = 2.9254 − .00040 CH − .12045 LOCH − .06418 SZF
       (.1114) (.00008)   (.0178)   (.01630)

Standard Deviation = .67288 R^2 = .1689

the model were compared with the original allocation results to test the "goodness of fit" of the model.

The second simulation simulated the increase in income of $1,000 by simply increasing the Y variable in equation (1) by $1,000 for black families. Completely effective open occupancy was produced by reducing the negative coefficient of −1.6279 for RACE in equation (2) to zero. The data for black families (61) was then run through the model of Table 5-1 with these changes made (i.e., two separate runs were made for the two policies) and the allocation results compared.

The third simulation, which reflected a change in accessibility, was produced by halfing the LOCW component of ACCTY (ACCTY = LOCW * Y) for those household heads who were employed in ring 1. The entire set of data was run through the model of Table 5-1 with the requisite changes made for those employed in ring 1. The allocation results for this simulation are compared with those of the first simulation to test the effectiveness of the change in accessibility.

The fourth simulation required the construction of two additional regression models: one based on data from rings 1 and 2 (city only) and one based on data from ring 3 (suburb only). The entire set of data was then run through both regression models and the results compared.

ANALYSIS OF SIMULATIONS

The analysis of variance about the mean was the test applied to these simulations to determine whether (1) the results produced were different from the original data; or (2) the two different alternative simulations were significantly different (e.g., open occupancy versus increased income for simulation two). Table 5-2

Table 5–2.   Analysis of Variance Format for Simulation Comparisons

$$F \;=\; \frac{MS_p}{MS_E} \quad \text{where:}$$

Source of Variation	Sum of Squares	Degrees of Freedom	Mean Square
BETWEEN RESULTS	SSresults $= n \sum\limits_{j=i}^{k} (\overline{X}_j - \overline{X})^2$	$k - 1$	MS_p = SSresults$/k - 1$
ERROR	SSresults $= \sum\limits_{i=1}^{n} \sum\limits_{j=1}^{k} (X_{ij} - X)$	$k(n-1)$	MS_E = SSresults$/k(n-1)$
TOTAL	SSresults $= \sum\limits_{i=1}^{n} \sum\limits_{j=1}^{k} (X_{ij} - \overline{X})^2$	$nk - 1$	

$\overline{X}_j$ =   mean of $j'th$ plan;

$\overline{X}$ =   grand mean;

k =   no. of simulations being compared;

n =   number in sample size;

H_O =   Result$_1$ = Result$_2$ = ... ;

If $F \geq F \propto {}_{\bullet} k - 1 {}_{\bullet} k(n-1)$ reject H_O; otherwise accept H_O.

Source: Thomas Naylor, Kenneth Werty, and Thomas Wannocott, "Methods for Analyzing Data From Compute Simulation," *Communications of the ACM,* Vol. 10, No. 11, November 1967.

indicates the general form of the F-test employed. In general, the null hypothesis that is being tested is H_O: Result$_1$ = Result$_2$ = Result$_3$ . . . . For example, the results for the open occupancy policy simulation (Result$_1$) are compared with the results for the increased income simulation (Result$_2$). If the F value yielded by the comparison of the simulation results exceeds the tabular value (based on level of confidence desired and the degrees of freedom in the numerator and denominator respectively) as obtained from a standard statistical table of F values the null hypothesis is rejected, which indicates that the results compared are significantly different (at the given level of confidence $\propto$).

COMMENTS ON DATA PROBLEMS

In examining the actual performance of the model with its various parameters, equations, and simulations, it is important to note that the estimation of the parameters involved data that reflect both the forces of supply and demand even though the basic model itself is demand oriented. Whether the city or its resultant data were in equilibrium or disequilibrium (most likely), the forces of both demand and supply were at work to produce the actual data that is used. For example, it may be that at a going rate or price for single-family structures in a given area, one hundred more were being demanded than existed with the resultant effect of a rationing process occurring either of a market (price) or a non-market nature (choosing only a particular type owner, and so on). The families in the queue will, in the interim before they are selected, be living in other structures of the same or different type and probably in a different area. In other words, the data did not reveal what their actual desires or demands are but rather what pertained at the time of data collection, which then becomes, for all practical purposes, their effective demand. Exactly what damage this does to the model is uncertain. Further, due to the crosssectional nature of the data, as household characteristics are changed, the behavior of the household is assumed to simulate that of a household presently embodying that characteristic—that is, if a household of a given size, race, and so forth has an increase in income, the model predicts that they will act in the same manner as that group of households (all other things being equal) that presently enjoys that level of income. The same type of procedure holds for other changes, such as in family size, age of the head of the household, and so on. Based on this particular behavioral assumption, the model is probably not too inaccurate in its analysis.

The issue does become crucial though when simulations are performed and certain subsequent predictions made. Here too it is more crucial when such variables as race are being analyzed than it would be if age were the variables in question. Despite these limitations, it is still possible to conduct meaningful simulation experiments by altering the variables in the demand-oriented model. The main reason for this is that although the supply function for housing varies greatly over time, which makes its estimation extremely difficult, the demand function has remained relatively constant both in terms of shape and position (i.e., shifts are quite predictable). Thus, simulated changes will follow a fairly distinct pattern, with these simulated patterns corresponding to empirically observed patterns of past behavior. Consequently, the estimated parameters based on equilibrium data can also be interpreted as closely approximating desired as well as actual demand.[1]

SIMULATION RESULTS

Having made these preliminary modifications and comments, we can now proceed on to the actual performance of the model. In order to simulate the data, it was necessary to construct a rather simple Fortran program to perform the simulations and to analyze some of the simulation results in terms of the F-test. A flow diagram of the program appears in Figure 5–1.

Figure 5–1. Flow Diagram of Fortran Program.

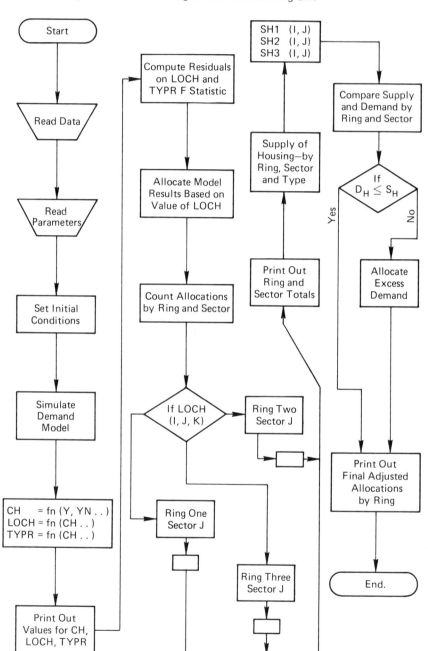

Figure 5–2. Map of Buffalo—Rings and Sectors.

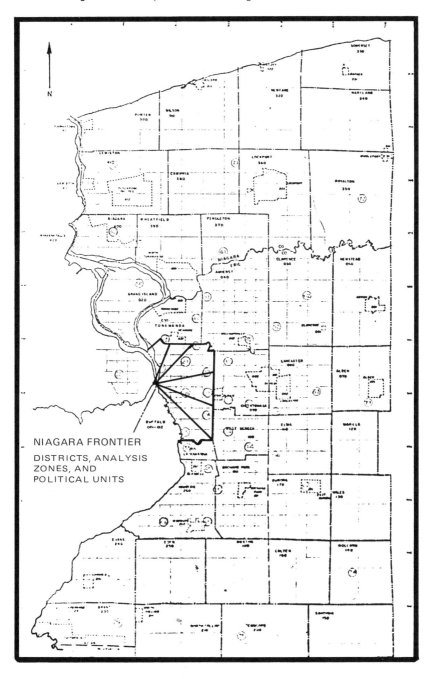

NIAGARA FRONTIER

DISTRICTS, ANALYSIS
ZONES, AND
POLITICAL UNITS

In examining the outputs and adjustments from the model, it should be noted that the sample data were from three distinct rings. Ring 1 (see Figure 5–1), which included the black ghetto, was, in general, the oldest residential areas in Buffalo and was represented by 177 households. Ring 2, which included the remaining areas of Buffalo, had the highest population total of all the rings and was represented by 203 households. Ring 3 included the oldest suburbs surrounding Buffalo and was represented by 190 households. Since the model is concerned mostly with locating households by type of dwelling unit, it is also necessary to indicate the original allocation of household by type, which is done in Table 5–3.

Simulation 1: Simple Run through the Demand Model, No Supply Adjustments

A simple run through the demand sector of the model with the data produced the results shown in Tables 5–4 and 5–5. The most dramatic shift from a purely allocational aspect occurred with regard to rings 1 and 2 in that the model shifted most of the white residents originally located in ring 1 to ring 2 with the remainder going to ring 3. The implications of this are that as time passes the central part of the city will be dominated by non-whites (blacks and browns) with the resulting movement of whites producing dramatic in-

Table 5–3. Supply of Housing, by Type and by Rings and Sectors, Buffalo

Rings	Sectors	SH1	SH2	SH3
Ring 1	1	25.00	37.00	37.00
	2	10.00	14.00	5.00
	3	8.00	18.00	19.00
	4	5.00	5.00	5.00
Ring 2	1	11.00	9.00	6.00
	2	7.00	14.00	3.00
	3	18.00	37.00	3.00
	4	15.00	32.00	10.00
	5	12.00	17.00	3.00
	6	5.00	5.00	3.00
Ring 3	1	12.00	17.00	5.00
	2	26.00	23.00	4.00
	3	17.00	11.00	6.00
	4	18.00	5.00	3.00
	5	17.00	5.00	3.00
	6	17.00	7.00	4.00

Note: SH1 = Supply of Single-Family Houses.
     SH2 = Supply of Two-Family Houses.
     SH3 = Supply of Multi-Family Houses.

Table 5–4. Simulation 1: Simple Run, Buffalo *(Allocation of Households by Ring and Sector)*

Ring	Sector	Model Allocating	Original Allocation
1	1	1	98
1	2	24	29
1	3	29	45
1	4	4 (58)	5 (177)
2	1	108	26
2	2	34	24
2	3	65	57
2	4	53	58
2	5	24	30
2	6	10 (294)	8 (203)
3	1	50	34
3	2	48	53
3	3	41	33
3	4	27	22
3	5	26	20
3	6	26 (218)	28 (190)
		570	570

Note: Of 61 persons allocated to ring 1, 59 are blacks; 6 other blacks are in (2. –2.) ring 2, sector 2.
Totals per ring are in parentheses.

Table 5–5. Simulation 1: Simple Run, Housing, by Type and by Sector, Buffalo

Ring	Sector	Type 1		Type 2		Type 3	
		Model	Original	Model	Original	Model	Original Allocation
1	1	0	25	1	37	0	37
1	2	4	10	16	14	6	5
1	3	2	8	18	18	10	19
1	4	0 (6)	5 (48)	5 (40)	5 (74)	0 (16)	5 (66)
2	1	28	11	76	9	5	6
2	2	10	7	24	14	1	3
2	3	11	18	55	37	0	3
2	4	13	15	39	32	2	10
2	5	11	12	14	17	0	3
2	6	2 (75)	5 (68)	9 (217)	5 (114)	0 (6)	3 (28)
3	1	40	12	11	17	0	5
3	2	40	26	9	23	0	4
3	3	36	17	6	11	0	6
3	4	22	18	6	5	0	3
3	5	21	17	6	5	0	3
3	6	24 (183)	17 (107)	3 (41)	7 (68)	0 (0)	4 (25)

Note: Totals by ring are in parentheses.

creases in the density of the outer fringes of the city and the suburbs. Certainly, there is nothing that is very startling about the first half of the prediction concerning black dominance in an ever widening central city belt. What has not been given as much attention is the dramatic rise in density that the outer areas of the city will experience since it is usually assumed that the flight will result only in an increase in suburban population. However, this ignores the very important dual problem of the household's budget constraint confronting sharp rises in suburban land prices as suburban population density rises—that is, although many white families would prefer to flee to the safety of the suburbs, they will not have the economic means to do so since their desire to move was not engendered by a rise in income but rather by a desire to exclude themselves from non-whites.[a] Hence, faced with the economic reality of rising prices for suburban land (and homes), they will have no choice but to settle in the outer areas of the city itself, which may produce the paradoxical result that for certain comparable type of homes (preferred by middle-income families) the price may be lower for non-whites (within the expanding frontier of the non-white ghetto) than for whites, which Becker and others have discovered.[2]

The most surprising result was the almost total absence of type three (multi-family) dwellings attributed to the various households. In analyzing this, one easy way out would be to assert that in reallocating households from ring 1 to rings 2 and 3, it was necessary to simultaneously change housing type as well (for those inhabiting type three dwellings that were mainly located in ring 1) since there were very few type three dwellings available in rings 2 and 3. However, the complete explanation is undoubtedly more complex than this. It most likely involves the way in which imputed rents were originally assigned, which may have not simulated the actual relative measures between rents actually paid by apartment dwellers and imputed rents of homeowners. In addition, it involves the desire of many apartment dwellers to move up the housing scale to either a two-family or single-family structure, but who cannot because enough are not available at the prevailing price. This is particularly crucial in that the type of dwelling assigned by the model (TYPR) is in the form of a continuous distribution yielding such numbers as 1.214, 1.318, 2.415, 3.112, and so forth, which are converted to a particular dwelling type (see Fortran program), whereas the actual housing market is a discrete distribution where the movement from one type of dwelling to another usually involves large magnitudinal changes of one sort or another (e.g., large increases in income or long periods of saving or changes in family structure). Since employment is also quite high in ring 2 (see

a. This is not to deny the existence of a rent gradient that continually declines as one proceeds out from the CBD but rather that suburban development is often constrained by zoning restrictions that do not allow densities above a certain level (or necessitate construction of single-family homes on a specified lot size), which precludes densities from adjusting to land prices. Therefore, a family who cannot afford a single-family unit in the suburbs may be precluded from locating there at all.

Chapter Four), this acts as another force attracting residents although its exact effects are difficult to determine since the accessibility measure used includes both income and distance to work. The final result the model yields in terms of housing type is probably a result of the interplay of these causes. In spite of this, the model still must be considered a partial failure for the very low figure it yields for multi-family structures (i.e., the directions indicated by the qualifications are correct but they still do not account for the magnitudes involved). This particular failure becomes more important in view of the increases in density predicted for ring 2, which should lead to a rise in multi-family dwellings resulting from higher land prices. The way to depict this would be in a truly dynamic model, which this is not since even after certain adjustments are made due to present supply constraints, there is still not a sufficient number of multi-family dwellings. Hence, one must be very careful in interpreting the results of a static model that cannot reflect dynamic processes and adjustments. In retrospect, though, perhaps it is enough for this model to predict a raise in density for the outer areas of the city and allow the policy maker or planner to either interpret them carefully or change certain parameters and run the model again.

F-Test on Simulation 1 for the Means of LOCH and TYPR. The first simulation test performed was one which examined whether the results produced by the recursive model for variables LOCH and TYPR were significantly different from the results produced by the regression equations for these variables. The method used to determine this is the analysis of variance and the test is the F-test. The assumptions underlying the valid use of the F-test are (a) independence of the statistical errors, (b) equality of variance, and (c) normality.[3]

The first condition is satisfied by the fact that the model is being driven by its exogenous variables, which can be assumed to be independent by virtue of the crosssectional nature of the data. As for the second condition, the standard deviation for the second equation or LOCH using the resgresion results was 1.4398 and for the recursive results was 1.4591. Similarly for TYPR, its regression standard deviation was .6725 and its recursive model's standard deviation was .6738. In both cases, the results are close enough to satisfy the second criterion. The third condition is satisfied by the robustness of the F-tests on the three regression equations which are respectively: (1) for CH, $F(3,566) = 708.8259$, (2) for LOCH, $F(5,564) = 358.8719$, and (3) for TYPR, $F(3,566) = 39.5533$.

The results of the F-test for the analysis of variance are shown in Table 5–6, which indicates that the results for LOCH (at both the .01 and .05 levels) is significantly different for the recursive model versus the regression, whereas the opposite is true for TYPR (i.e., the null hypothesis is supported). A reasonable explanation is that LOCH contains more independent variables than does TYPR, which allows more room for variance. However, there is a flaw in

Table 5-6. Simulation 1: Simple Test of Model, Analysis of Variance for LOCH and TYPR, Buffalo

Variable	Source of Variation	Sum of Squares	Degrees of Freedom	Mean Square
LOCH	BETWEEN	3.6418	1	3.6418
TYPR	RESULTS	.2592	1	.2592
LOCH		251.9532	1138	.2214
	ERROR			
TYPR		133,1218	1138	.1161
LOCH		255.5950	1139	
	TOTAL			
TYPR		133.3800	1139	

F(LOCH) = 16.4523

F(TYPR) = 2.2329

F_{05} (1,1138) = 3.84

F_{01} (1,1138) = 6.64

Source: Samuel Richmond, *Statistical Analysis* (Ronald Press, New York, 1965), p. 580.

this in that CH and LOCH combined are more important in TYPR than is CH in LOCH, but their combined effects may somewhat cancel out in TYPR to produce a closer correspondence with the regression results. In short, the statistical probability is that TYPR would have a higher *F* value than LOCH but that empirically the opposite result holds.

Results of Supply Constraint. The next task was to examine the results of the model after the adjustments were made that reflect the supply constraints imposed upon the demand sector of the model. Table 5-7 indicates the supply constraints imposed by the model. Rather than following the constraints perfectly, which would tend to duplicate the original model allocations, the following adjustment rules were followed. In the case of excess demand, for ring 2, if the household were white, the even numbered households in the sample were allowed to remain but their housing type (TYPR) was augmented by one (increase in density). The odd numbered households were allocated one half to the ring (sector remained constant) preceding it geographically (i.e., ring 2's excess to ring 1) and one half to the ring following it geographically or to another sector if a vacancy existed (with housing type remaining constant). For ring 3, housing type and sector allocation remained constant with one half the excess being allocated to ring 4 (i.e., further out) unless the desired housing existed in another sector of ring 3. Blacks were not allowed to move and adjustments for them were made by augmenting or decreasing housing type where necessary. The adjusted results are shown in Tables 5-8 and 5-9. If ring 3 did follow either the exact adjustment mechanism of ring 2 or with some of the

Table 5–7. Simulation 1: Supply of Housing, by Type and by Ring and Sector, Buffalo

Ring	Sector	Type 1	Type 2	Type 3
1	1	14	30	21
1	2	13	21	16
1	3	13	26	18
1	4	3	5	7
2	1	14	16	9
2	2	15	13	5
2	3	16	21	11
2	4	20	29	10
2	5	13	11	4
2	6	7	7	4
3	1	15	14	4
3	2	23	30	7
3	3	15	14	5
3	4	14	5	2
3	5	14	3	2
3	6	14	10	2

Note: Type 1 = Single-Family Homes.
Type 2 = Two-Family Dwellings.
Type 3 = Multi-Family Dwellings.

excess going to ring 1 directly, the final result would show a more significant build-up in ring 1, but this was not done because it makes the adjustment mechanism very complex and because it riggs the results to closely correspond with the original allocation, which then ignores possible errors in the predictions of the model.

The main adjustment, in terms of numbers, comes with a net redistribution of households from ring 2 to ring 1 and from ring 3 to ring 4. Ring 2 continues to dominate, but at least the distribution has become more skewed and more reasonable. As for distribution of housing types, this mainly involved shifting an excess demand for a two-family dwellings from ring 2 to ring 1 and an excess demand for single-family dwellings from ring 3 to ring 4. The model continues to fail in its ability to assign families to multi-family dwellings for reasons discussed previously. Even with the adjustments, though, ring 2 is still much too dominant and ring 1 much too sparsely populated. Yet, if one were to peer into the future, the increase in population in ring 1 will not come from the families now located there (except for blacks) as these will be moving into rings 2 and 3 as the model predicts, but from immigration, increases in present non-white population, from older couples returning to the central city after their children have grown (e.g., Carl Sandburg Village in Chicago) and by young singles and young married couples desiring to be close to their jobs and entertainment centers (e.g., Bunker Hill project in Los Angeles). As it now exists, the

Table 5–8.   Simulation 1: Simple Run, Adjustment for Supply
Constraint, Allocation of Households, Buffalo

Ring	Sector	No.
1	1	15
1	2	28
1	3	38
1	4	5 (86)
2	1	62
2	2	34
2	3	53
2	4	58
2	5	30
2	6	18 (255)
3	1	45
3	2	48
3	3	36
3	4	24
3	5	22
3	6	26 (201)
4	1	6
4	2	4
4	3	5
4	4	4
4	5	4
4	6	5 (28)
		570

model is incapable of testing these latter two contentions. In order to do so, the data for older couples and young singles and young marrieds would have to be taken out and run separately.

In summary, then, even after adjustments are made, the model's distribution still deviates radically from the original allocation in terms of the dominance of ring 2 (which is directionally valid but magnitudinally biased upwards) and of the dearth of multi-family dwellings, which is patently untrue due to the inability of the model to reflect certain crucial economic factors such as the response to increased demand for land.

Simulation 2: Open Occupancy versus
Increased Income for Blacks

The first policy simulation run with the model involves the race variable. The first half of the simulation involves changing the coefficient on the RACE variable from −1.6278 to zero, which implies a completely successful open-occupancy policy. The second half involves arbitrarily increasing black's level of income by $1,000, which simultaneously affects both location (LOCH)

Table 5-9. Simulation 1: Simple Run, Adjustment for Supply Constraint, by Housing Type, Buffalo

Ring	Sector	Type #1	Type #2	Type #3
1	1	4	12	0
1	2	4	19	6
1	3	2	27	10
1	4	0	5	0
2	1	20	35	8
2	2	13	18	4
2	3	16	27	11
2	4	20	34	5
2	5	13	14	4
2	6	4	11	4
3	1	28	14	4
3	2	32	14	3
3	3	25	11	1
3	4	18	5	2
3	5	18	3	2
3	6	19	8	0
4	1	6	0	0
4	2	4	0	0
4	3	5	0	0
4	4	4	0	0
4	5	4	0	0
4	6	5	0	0

and type of dwelling inhabited (TYPR). In order to perform these simulations using the coefficients for the entire model, it is necessary to assume that blacks will behave the same as whites who are in the sample. The validity of this assumption can be partially tested by comparing the regression results for the entire model with that for blacks alone. However, there is a pitfall here in that one can argue that blacks do tend to act the same as whites as income rises and certain racial constraints removed. Since this is exactly what this particular set of simulations is concerned with, the comparison of regression coefficients will only give a partial hint as to validity of the simulation.

The regression results for blacks alone are shown in Table 5-10. A cursory examination indicates the results are radically different than the results for the entire sample particularly with reference to the values of the coefficients and their respective "*t*"-values. The underlying statistical relations, which produced this set of regression results can be determined by viewing the correlation matrix (see Table 5-11). Rather than discussing the differences variable by variable, only the significant differences both with respect to statistical and predictive implications will be examined. The first equation gives the dominant role to income to an even greater extent than did the entire model. However, its

Table 5–10. Simulation 2: Regression Results for Blacks Only, Buffalo

(1)   CH   =   331.6354   +   .1566 Y   −   .0331 YN   +   1.0625 OCCUP
          (76.7285)   (.0074)   (.0170)   (31.2894)

   Standard Deviation = 126.5508 R^2 = .8659

(2)   LOCH =   .7657   +   .000056 CH   +   .00018 YN   +   .0197 RACE
          (.1020)   (.000058)   (.00002)   (.0377)

          +   .0324 MODE   +   .00025 ACCTY
              (.0423)   (.00111)

   Standard Deviation = .1497 R^2 = .5310

(3)   TYPR =   3.508   −   .0151 SZF   −   .00032 CH   −   .6100 LOCH
          (.6898)   (.0436)   (.00026)   (.4160)

   Standard Deviation = .7792 R^2 = .0287

exact influence is clouded by its multi-collinearity problems with respect to YN, which has produced the perplexing negative sign on this variable. In general, the final results numerically break down as follows: blacks spend approximately 20 percent more on housing than do whites with similar income. For the second equation the most significant difference is the minor role played by the RACE variable, which is due to the fact that the entire sample is black (except for 5 households). Hence, this equation is not really a valid one to use in any simulation in which interaction occurs with whites. The third equation is interesting because the only significant variable is the constant. Table 5–11 indicates that instead of CH and LOCH, such variables as age and Y (income) should have been used. Despite these major differences, the actual numbers produced by the equations, when used with the boundaries of the simulation model for both LOCH and TYPR, do not yield results dramatically different than the original model yielded. Because of this and more importantly because of the problems involved in re-estimating a model that would have the same significant variables for entire model and the "blacks only" model (which is necessary for meaningful simulation comparisons), it was decided that the coefficients for the entire model would be used. The working assumption for this to hold would be one that implies that as constraints are removed from blacks, they will tend to act as their white counterparts. This tendency is actually built into the coefficients of the entire model since they contain both black and white households, with the majority being white. It is further felt that both the actual numerical results of the simulation (using entire model's coefficients) and their implications bear out the validity of this assumption and the subsequent approach.

   The results for the simulations using the coefficients for the entire model are shown in Table 5–12. The major effect of the $1,000 increase in

Table 5–11.   Simulation 2: Correlation Matrix for Blacks Only, Buffalo

	TYPR	SZF	PCAR	Y	YN	CH	AGE	RACE	OCCUP	MODE	LOCH	LOCW
SZF	-0.07											
PCAR	-0.06	0.18										
Y	-0.23	0.16	0.53									
YN	-0.24	0.03	0.01	0.31								
CH	-0.19	0.14	0.44	0.93	0.21							
AGE	-0.29	-0.30	-0.01	-0.11	-0.08	-0.09						
RACE	-0.12	0.08	-0.12	-0.00	0.12	0.00	-0.19					
OCCUP	-0.14	-0.07	0.34	0.23	0.02	0.22	0.08	0.30				
MODE	-0.01	-0.00	0.29	0.24	-0.21	0.28	0.03	0.00	0.09			
LOCH	-0.21	0.06	0.04	0.34	0.74	0.27	0.03	0.13	0.09	-0.05		
LOCW	-0.19	-0.05	-0.04	0.05	-0.08	0.14	0.16	-0.17	-0.06	0.28	0.02	
ACCTY	-0.21	-0.02	0.13	0.41	0.02	0.47	0.09	-0.17	0.03	0.39	0.10	0.88

Table 5–12. Simulation 2: Comparing Difference between Increased Income for Blacks versus Open Occupancy, Buffalo

Ring	Sector	Original	Model	Y Increased by $1000	Open Occupancy
1	1	0	0	0	0
1	2	25	24	21	0
1	3	28	29	28	0
1	4	2	4	4	0
2	1	0	0	0	0
2	2	5	6	8	20
2	3	1	0	1	26
2	4	3	0	1	4
2	5	0	0	0	0
2	6	0	0	0	0
3	2	0	0	0	10
3	3	0	0	0	3

Blacks–TYPR–Type of Residence

Ring	Sector	Original			Model			Y Increased by $1000			Open Occupancy		
		Housing Type											
		1	2	3	1	2	3	1	2	3	1	2	3
1	1	0	0	0	0	0	0	0	0	0	0	0	0
1	2	8	14	3	6	12	6	8	10	3	0	0	0
1	3	4	13	11	3	15	11	6	14	8	0	0	0
1	4	1	0	1	0	4	0	2	2	0	0	0	0
2	1	0	0	0	0	0	0	0	0	0	0	0	0
2	2	1	4	0	2	4	0	3	5	0	5	11	2
2	3	1	0	0	0	0	0	1	0	0	3	12	9
2	4	0	3	0	0	0	0	1	0	0	1	3	1
2	5	0	0	0	0	0	0	0	0	0	0	0	0
2	6	0	0	0	0	0	0	0	0	0	1	2	2
3	2	0	0	0	0	0	0	0	0	0	3	7	2

income was not an allocational one but rather a qualitative one in which blacks remained in approximately the same geographical positions as before but improved their housing quality (i.e., increase in quality is tantamount to change in housing occupied) by reducing their consumption of two-family and multi-family unit services and increasing their consumption of single-family unit services. Alternatively, the main effect of the open occupancy simulation was to dramatically alter the allocational pattern of blacks by removing them completely from ring 1 and allocating them to rings 2 and 3, with the majority going to ring 2 (note: housing type or quality remained basically constant in this simulation).

One must be careful, though, in interpreting the results of these simulations. A cursory glance would indicate that the best way to break up the ghetto would be to pass and then fully enforce an open occupancy law rather than increasing black incomes through the use of a negative income tax or some other subsidy. In making this policy presumption based on the simulation results of the model, the practitioner would be well advised to recall some basic economics particularly with regard to demand and supply. It is probably true that as the simulation indicates, increases in incomes to blacks are not in themselves (unless they were unreasonably large) sufficient to break up the ghetto. Particularly in cities such as Buffalo where the race constraint appears to be very strong, an incomes policy favoring blacks (i.e., low-income groups) might increase the rents paid by blacks with no complementary increase in housing services consumed either in the form of improved dwellings or lower densities because quantities demanded would be increasing faster than quantities supplied, which may only be a short-run phenomenon depending on the price elasticity of the supply of housing. This could happen because the supply of new dwellings plus the supply of homes being sold by whites would not be sufficient to satisfy the new level of demand based on the new levels of subsidized incomes. The modifying influence here is the increased ability of blacks with their new higher subsidized levels of income to bid away resources from the white community for the building of new homes and for bidding away existing dwellings on the borders between black and white renters and homeowners. In short, an increase in income even without an open-occupancy law would enable blacks to increase their housing supply at a faster rate than at present due to their new relative (vis-à-vis whites) increase in purchasing power, but the net effect would probably be an across-the-board increase in rents for all concerned, due to quantities demanded exceeding even the increased quantities supplied.

Similarly, the constraint on the effectiveness of a successful open-occupancy law is whether the blacks could afford the new types of housing now open to them. The model itself partially indicates this on both the demand and supply side by showing that as one goes out from the CBD, housing becomes less dense and generally of higher quality. Therefore, without increasing the purchasing power of blacks, an open-occupancy law can become a source of frustration and certainly a moot policy if no substantial changes in allocation or location result from its existence unless we assume blacks now pay so much more for comparable housing than do whites that all that is needed is the removal of this social barrier. This is probably the case to some degree (recall Becker's exception though), but certainly not to the point where it would negate the previous discussion.

It appears then that what is needed is a combination of an income policy and an open-occupancy law if ghettoes are to be effectively broken up. It will depend on the particular city involved (or even the particular area in a city) as to which should be emphasized more as this involves not only the economic factors already mentioned but also the desires of the community itself. A cost-effectiveness approach may be useful with weights being assigned to the various costs and benefits in order to reflect the community's desires. In the case of Buffalo, assuming the break-up of the ghetto is the dominant goal, the greater emphasis should be placed on the open-occupancy aspect of the policy. This is evident from the simulation results as stated in Table 5–12 and also from the F-tests between the two policies as they effect location and type of dwelling occupied (as shown in Table 5–13), which indicates that the greatest difference occurs in the LOCH or locational variable. However, even with the proper balance of open occupancy and income policy, it may be necessary for the market to be stimulated in some way to effect an increase in the supply of housing (e.g., by legislating uniform codes that permit mass construction techniques, and so forth), or the program will result more in a bidding up of the price of housing rather than increased quantities for both blacks and whites, which will have substantial "back-lash" effects on both sides.

A final note of caution should be sounded with respect to simulations that incorporate both policies of open occupancy and increased income— that is, unless one has a truly dynamic model for these simulations, the final results of any policy variables will depend upon their dynamic interaction, which is greatly influenced by the interaction of the forces shaping quantities demanded and quantities supplied. The actual simulation experiment, if carefully constructed and interpreted, can indicate directions of variables and movements to them, but can rarely indicate exact magnitudes (in the arena of urban activity) and should not, at this stage of development, be expected to do so.

Table 5–13. Simulation 2: Open Occupancy versus Increased Income for Blacks, Analysis of Variance for LOCH and TYPR, Buffalo

Variable	Source of Variation		Sum of Squares	Degrees of Freedom	Mean Square
LOCH	BETWEEN		74.1900	1	74.1900
TYPR	RESULTS		.6148	1	.6148
LOCH	ERROR		178.8936	1138	.1572
TYPR			52.2826	1138	.0477
LOCH			253.0836	1139	
TYPR		TOTAL	52.8974	1139	

F(LOCH) = 472.9059
F(TYPR) =   12.8805

Simulation 3: Change in Accessibility
to Ring 1

The next simulation is concerned with how changes in accessibility affect location. Specifically, the accessibility to the central business district and surrounding area (basically ring 1) was increased by halving the t (t = distance from CBD for place of work) value for this area in the accessibility variable ACCTY (equation two). A priori, there are two possible effects of this change in accessibility. The first would involve an increase in density for ring 1 because it was now more accessible (i.e., accessibility is a two-way street). The second possibility, which is the opposite of the first, is that greater accessibility to any particular area permits a lowering of densities in surrounding areas since one can get to the desired area in the same amount of time as previously but with an increase in distance from it. Once again, however, both these effects are over-simplified and do not accurately reflect all the complex phenomena that would operate to produce or modify them. Yet, both indicate major directions of change that might take place.

Of these two possibilities, the second is the most interesting. It implies that if a city were to build more expressways to its central business district, the result might be to increase urban sprawl, which often necessitates the further construction of freeways and/or ends up choking the central city with traffic, which would inhibit its further economic growth. If rapid transit is built instead and accessibility improved via this mechanism, the sprawl will occur but there will probably be no adverse affects upon the central business district itself. If urban sprawl is viewed as undesirable, the correct policy prescription is to do nothing at all (i.e., avoid second effect), which will, if present trends continue, eventually make it so costly to drive to work in the CBD or other similar areas that employers will disperse to areas where they are closer to their workers and workers will be forced to relocate close to the CBD (e.g., Bunker Hill Residential Project in downtown Los Angeles), which areas they had originally abandoned. Both of these trends, which are responses to present congestion, appear to be "good" for the worker since they shorten his journey-to-work in both time and distance and thus give him more leisure time. If this is so, then cities certainly do themselves harm by building more expressways and perhaps even by building more rapid transit facilities, although the results are not so obvious here.

In the case of Buffalo, the allocational effects of an increase in accessibility to ring 1 are shown in Tables 5-14 and 5-15. Its effect, at best, is negligible as only a net total of 9 households are relocated (of a possible 570), which is due to the small role that the distance variable plays in the accessibility function (i.e., ACCTY = Y * LOCW). However, if the change in variables is examined more closely the direction of change is toward more concentration in ring 1, which indicates that in this case, this may be an effective countermeasure

Table 5-14. Simulation 3: Change in Work Accessibility to Ring 1, Allocation of Households, Buffalo

Ring	Sector	Original	Adjusted Model[a]	Simple Model[a]	Increase In Accessibility
1	1	98	16	1	1
1	2	29	29	25	27
1	3	45	39	30	30
1	4	5	5	5	5
2	1	26	63	109	115
2	2	24	35	35	34
2	3	57	54	66	66
2	4	58	59	54	54
2	5	30	31	25	25
2	6	8	19	11	11
3	1	34	46	51	45
3	2	53	49	49	48
3	3	33	37	42	42
3	4	22	25	28	28
3	5	20	23	27	27
3	6	28	27	27	27
4	1		6		
4	2		4		
4	3		5		
4	4		4		
4	5		4		
4	6		5		

a. Refers to Table 5-8.
b. Refers to Table 5-4.

Table 5-15. Simulation 3: Change in Accessibility to Ring 1, Analysis of Variance for LOCH, Buffalo

Variable	Source of Variation	Sum of Squares	Degrees of Freedom	Mean Square
LOCH	BETWEEN RESULTS	.2592	1	.2592
	ERROR	.2862	1138	.2862
	TOTAL	.5454	1139	

F(LOCH) = .9056

to urban sprawl. Here again, though, the limitations of this type of simulation become apparent, which is due to the previously discussed limitations on the accessibility function or variable and the ignoring of functional supply constraints. More specifically, what sort of locational changes would be effected by a changing structure of land prices in ring 1 as it became more accessible? Would, it be enough to alter the original prediction of an increase in residential density, which was the result of our "ceteris paribus" assumption? Although most models and most economic theory use this type of assumption, its usefulness and practicality became much more limited when dealing with problems of simulation that employ simple models to reflect complex phenomena.

Simulation 4: Allocation by City versus Suburban Models

The final simulation is concerned with comparing and analyzing the regression models and their subsequent allocations for city dwellers alone (rings 1 and 2) and suburban dwellers (ring 3). This is done in order to better assess future household movements. Do we view present suburban dwellers as the most accurate predictor of what is to come, or do we look at city dwellers and project what now pertains for them? Are the two results significantly different? If they are, which seems more reasonable? Rather than choosing, should we simply adhere to the present models predictions which are a combination of the two? A priori we would expect the "city only" model to produce less dispersed results than either the original or "suburban only" model and vice versa for the "suburban only" model.

The regression results for the two models are shown in Tables 5–16

Table 5–16. Simulation 4: Regression Results for Rings 1 and 2, Buffalo

(1) $CH = 289.6470 + .1068$ Y $+ .0184$ YN $+ 51.3752$ OCCUP
(49.9498) $(.0035)$ $(.0093)$ (18.1538)

Standard Deviation = 170.6233 $R^2 = .7673$

(2) $LOCH = .2387 + .00045$ YN $- .00031$ CH $- .4245$ RACE
$(.2907)$ $(.00004935)$ $(.00014)$ $(.1264)$

$+ .0141$ MODE $+ .0068$ ACCTY
$(.1200)$ $(.0018)$

Standard Deviation = .8356 $R^2 = .3095$

(3) $TYPR = 2.9995 - .06475$ SZF $- .00039$ CH $- .1546$ LOCH
$(.1471)$ $(.0200)$ $(.000101)$ $(.03534)$

Standard Deviation = .1682 $R^2 = .1240$

Table 5–17.   Simulation 4: Regression Results for Ring 3, Buffalo

(1)	CH	=	336.09311	+ .1249 Y	+ .0051 YN	+	22.5734 OCCUP

(1)   CH   =   336.09311   + .1249 Y   + .0051 YN   +   22.5734 OCCUP
            (36.8273)   (.0041)   (.00267)   (22.397)

Standard Deviation = 145.5155 R^2 = .8376

(2)   LOCH =   5.4433   + .0009 YN   + .00006 CH   + .0952684 MODE
                (.15211)   (.0003)   (.00008)   (.11645)

            − .00009 ACCTY
              (.0011)

Standard Deviation = .3697 R^2 = .0200

(3)   TYPR =   3.625   − .0573 SZF   − .0004 CH   − .2415 LOCH
                (.7421)   (.0282)   (.0001)   (.1311)

Standard Deviation = .6566 R^2 = .0859

and 5–17. The only significant difference between the results for rings 1 and 2 and for all three rings occurs in equation (2) for the coefficient on the CH variable, which is negative here and positive (which we would expect) in the regression for all three rings. This can partially be explained by the potentially serious multi-collinearity problems between (see Table 5–18) CH and ACCTY (r of .42 versus r of .15 between CH and LOCH) and YN (r of .37). Other than this, the results are almost identical, particularly for equations (1) and (3), to the results from the entire sample. As for the regression results from ring 3, the major differences again occur in equation (2) (LOCH) in which the variables are not significant and ACCTY has a negative sign attached to it due possibly to multi-collinearity (Table 5–19) problems with CH (i.e., r of .44 between ACCTY and CH versus r of .03 between ACCTY and LOCH). RACE was not included in this equation as a variable since all households were white and thus in the simulations the variable is eliminated. Despite the fact that certain variables were not significant, all were included in the simulations for the sake of workable consistency and because predictions rather than analytics were what was being examined.

The allocational results for the two models are shown in Table 5–20. Not too surprisingly, the "city only" model allocates a larger proportion of households to the city with most of the increase occurring with allocations from ring 3 to ring 2 with very little increase for ring 1, which further reinforces the results of the "entire people" model, which also yielded a high concentration in ring 2. The "suburb only" results indicate that there are significant differences between their locational preferences and those of city dwellers in that all households were effectively located in ring 3. This seems to indicate that there are (together with the regression results) certain very essential variables that affect location for suburbanites, which are not included in this analysis. The F-tests

Table 5–18.   Simulation 4: Correlation Matrix for Rings 1 and 2, Buffalo

	TYPR	SZF	PCAR	Y	YN	CH	AGE	RACE	OCCUP	MODE	LOCH	LOCW
SZF	-0.20											
PCAR	-0.20	0.13										
Y	-0.21	0.10	0.39									
YN	-0.14	0.03	0.25	0.36								
CH	-0.24	0.11	0.38	0.87	0.37							
AGE	-0.13	-0.27	-0.03	0.03	-0.02	-0.00						
RACE	0.05	0.05	-0.20	-0.12	-0.40	-0.07	-0.09					
OCCUP	-0.00	-0.01	0.34	0.22	0.19	0.27	-0.04	-0.28				
MODE	-0.04	0.07	0.39	0.15	0.08	0.20	-0.10	-0.12	0.21			
LOCH	-0.26	0.09	0.18	0.24	0.52	0.15	-0.03	-0.35	0.15	0.08		
LOCW	-0.05	0.06	0.05	0.01	-0.01	0.03	-0.09	-0.01	0.12	0.19	0.11	
ACCTY	-0.14	0.06	0.20	0.48	0.15	0.42	-0.04	-0.06	0.16	0.19	0.21	0.80

Table 5–19. Simulation 4: Correlation Matrix for Ring 3, Buffalo

	TYPR	SZF	PCAR	Y	YN	CH	AGE	OCCUP	MODE	LOCH	LOCW
SZF	-0.19										
PCAR	-0.19	0.11									
Y	-0.10	0.11	0.26								
YN	-0.10	0.07	-0.09	-0.01							
CH	-0.24	0.14	0.31	0.91	0.04						
AGE	0.03	-0.31	-0.05	0.05	-0.02	0.00					
OCCUP	-0.08	-0.00	0.22	0.20	-0.07	0.21	-0.08				
MODE	-0.02	0.16	0.40	0.15	-0.25	0.14	-0.18	0.12			
LOCH	-0.16	0.12	0.02	0.02	0.01	0.07	-0.03	-0.14	0.06		
LOCW	-0.03	-0.01	0.12	0.02	-0.01	-0.00	-0.02	0.09	0.18	0.02	
ACCTY	-0.06	0.02	0.22	0.52	-0.03	0.44	0.04	0.17	0.18	0.03	0.82

Table 5–20. Simulation 4: City versus Suburb, Allocation Results, Buffalo

Ring	Sector	Original	Model[a]	City Only	Suburb Only
1	1	98	1	1	1
1	2	29	25	20	1
1	3	45	30	43	1
1	4	5	5	8	1
2	1	26	109	157	1
2	2	24	35	70	1
2	3	57	66	93	1
2	4	58	54	78	1
2	5	30	25	50	1
2	6	8	11	37	1
3	1	34	51	3	159
3	2	53	49	19	107
3	3	33	42	2	136
3	4	22	28	1	86
3	5	20	27	2	51
3	6	28	27	1	37

a. Simple Model refers to the results of the first simulation or Table 5–4.
Source: Samuel Richmond, *Statistical Analysis,* p. 580.

further confirm this fact (Table 5–21) since the *F*-test for LOCH between the simple model and "city only" is less than that between "city only" and "suburb only" (Table 5–22), although both are highly significant. Further, the *F*-tests for LOCH indicates that the null hypothesis for all three possibilities examined is refuted and each is a significantly different simulation.

No attempt has been made to dissect the results for the TYPR variable except the *F*-test (Tables 5–21, 5–22, and 5–23), which indicates that here too the simulation results for all three possibilities are significantly different.

What this particular set of simulations has shown is that one must be careful in projecting variables and their behavior over time for large areas or systems if the subareas or subsystems are not mere reflections of the entire area or system. This set of simulations also concludes the analysis of the Buffalo model and its workings.

In the next chapter, we turn to the city of Milwaukee to see what additional information can be obtained about residential location and then proceed to compare its results with those of Buffalo.

Table 5–21. Simulation 4: City versus Suburb, Analysis of Variance for LOCH and TYPR, Simple Model versus "City Only" Model, Buffalo

Variable	Source of Variation	Sum of Squares	Degrees of Freedom	Mean Square
LOCH	BETWEEN RESULTS	130.4987	1	130.4987
TYPR		1.4719	1	1.4719
LOCH		520.5112	1138	.9574
	ERROR			
TYPR		73.8562	1138	.0649
LOCH		651.0099	1139	
TYPR		75.3281	1139	

F(LOCH = 136.3038
F(TYPR) = 22.6854

Table 5–22. Simulation 4: City versus Suburb, Analysis of Variance for LOCH and TYPR, City Results versus Suburban Results, Buffalo

Variable	Source of Variation	Sum of Squares	Degrees of Freedom	Mean Square
LOCH	BETWEEN RESULTS	410.3977	1	410.3977
TYPR		20.5322	1	20.5322
	ERROR			
LOCH		916.094	1138	.8050
TYPR		73.970	1138	.0650
LOCH		1326.4917	1139	
	TOTAL			
TYPR		94.5022	1139	

F(LOCH) = 507.8232
F(TYPR) = 315.8657

Table 5–23. **Simulation 4: City versus Suburb, Analysis of Variance for LOCH and TYPR, Simple Results versus Suburb Results, Buffalo**

Variable	Source of Variation	Sum of Squares	Degrees of Freedom	Mean Square
LOCH	BETWEEN RESULTS	130.4987	1	130.4987
TYPR		1.4719	1	1.4719
LOCH		439.1584	1138	.3868
	ERROR			
TYPR		35.5642	1138	.0309
LOCH		569.6571	1139	
TYPR		37.0361	1139	

F(LOCH   = 337.3650
F(TYPR) =   45.5667

Chapter Six

The Milwaukee Model

ANALYSIS AND COMPARISON WITH BUFFALO MODEL

In analyzing the residential location patterns of the Milwaukee households, the same model and variables are employed that were used in the Buffalo analysis.[1] Consequently, only the major empirical differences between the two cities will be examined since the original reasons surrounding the inclusion of the present variables and the form of the model were discussed in Chapter Four. For illustrative purposes, Table 6–1 again presents the results of the Buffalo location model (using OLS). Tables 6–2 and 6–3 present the Milwaukee results for this same basic model. Table 6–2 represents the results using ordinary least squares

Table 6–1. Final Form of Buffalo Model, Including Accessibility Variable Regression Equations, Ordinary Least Squares

(1) $CH = 318.2539 + .1146\ Y + .0091\ YN + 48.1938\ OCCUP$
$(24.0803)\quad (.0026)\quad\ (.0028)\quad\quad (14.5263)$

Standard Deviation = 167.2499 $\quad\quad R^2 = .7887$

(2) $LOCH = 1.8790 + .00055\ CH + .00013\ YN - 1.6279\ RACE$
$(.2790)\quad\ (.00018)\quad\ (.000021)\quad\quad (.19632)$

$\quad\quad\quad + .3669\ MODE + .0058\ ACCTY$
$\quad\quad\quad\ (.1863)\quad\quad\ (.00247)$

Standard Deviation = 1.4341 $\quad\quad R^2 = .2346$

(3) $TYPR = 2.9254 - .00040\ CH - .12045\ LOCH - .06418\ SZF$
$(.1114)\quad\ (.00008)\quad\ (.0178)\quad\quad (.01630)$

Standard Deviation = .67288 $\quad\quad R^2 = .1689$

Table 6–2. Regression Results, Ordinary Least Squares, Rings 1, 2, and 3, Milwaukee

(1)   CH = − 64.02281   +   .13882   Y   +   .05773   YN   +   16.54871   OCCUP
            (47.9594)   (.0042)   (.0068)   (8.001)

      Standard Deviation = 301.1538 R^2 = .7410

(2)   LOCH = .66147   +   .00049   CH   +   .00032   YN   −   1.00107   RACE
             (.2455)   (.00011)   (.00003)   (.19828)

           +   .32302   MODE   +   .00665   ACCTY
               (.13375)   (.00247)

      Standard Deviation = 1.37083 R^2 = .3709

(3)   TYPR = 2.5723   −   .00017   CH   −   .10545   LOCH   −   .08843   SZF
           (.09654)   (.00005)   (.01743)   (.015539)

      Standard Deviation = .652317 R^2 = .1615

Table 6–3. Regression Results, Two-Stage Least Squares, Rings 1, 2, and 3, Milwaukee

(2)   LOCH = .6828   +   .00030   CH   −   .9967   RACE   +   .3417   MODE
           (.2450)   (.00014)   (1961)   (.1337)

           +   .00034   YN   +   .0079   ACCTY
               (.000036)   (.00255)

      Standard Deviation = 1.373 R^2 = .3684

(3)   TYPR = 2.7684   −   .00009   CH   −   .1816   LOCH   −   .0915   SZF
           (.1233)   (.00007)   (.0369)   (.01587)

      Standard Deviation = .6630 R^2 = .1336

to estimate the parameters, whereas Table 6–3 represents the parameters for equations (2) and (3) using two-stage least squares. Once again as with the Buffalo model, the two methods yield numerically different results for the coefficients but not significantly different predictions in terms of the actual numbers yielded for variables LOCH and TYPR. Hence, the analysis proceeds with a comparison between the results yielded by the ordinary least squares estimators (Tables 6–1 and 6–2).

For equation (1), there are no major differences between the two models either in the magnitudes of the parameters or their signs. Despite this fact, there remain some interesting contrasts. To begin with, the constant has changed from a very positive number of intercept (Buffalo) to a negative number (Milwaukee). It is also insignificant for Milwaukee but quite significant for

Buffalo. The income or Y variable is statistically more important (*"t"*-test) for Buffalo but numerically more important (.1388 versus .1146) for Milwaukee. The most significant difference between the two models is the variable YN. It is both statistically (*t*-value of 8.4 versus 3.2) and numerically (.057 versus .009) more important for Milwaukee than Buffalo. Thus, it appears that the Veblenesque influence (or "keeping up with the Jones'es") is more important for Milwaukee than Buffalo. Although the proxy variable OCCUP, for the lifetime expectation of earnings is statistically significant for Milwaukee (*t*-value of 2.071), its low numerical value of 16.5 indicates that it is doing a much poorer job of getting at this concept of expectation of earnings than it did for Buffalo, which even there was deemed inadequate in size. Therefore, it appears that some new variable must be found to account for this expectation of earnings or wealth effect.

Equation (2) for Milwaukee provides some interesting contrasts but also fails to change the basic patterns established by the Buffalo results. The constant for Milwaukee is much lower (.7 versus 1.8) than for Buffalo, which allows the independent variables to play a larger numerical role in explaining the actual geographic location of the residence (as linearly distant from the CBD). CH plays basically the same statistical and numerical role in both cities. The YN variable is also more important, both statistically and numerically, for Milwaukee than Buffalo, which implies there is more class clustering by income type in Milwaukee than Buffalo. This may, in turn, imply that ethnic class forces are not as important in Milwaukee as are income class forces. The RACE variable takes on a lesser role, numerically and statistically, in Milwaukee than Buffalo although it retains its negative sign. A major contrast between Milwaukee and Buffalo in terms of the roles that YN and RACE play in this particular equation is that such class variables as ethniticity and RACE are reversed in importance, with the income class variable YN being more important for Milwaukee. This may indicate that Milwaukee has evolved further sociologically than Buffalo. However, this is only a suggestion and not a positive assertion as it is only one possible interpretation of these results.

Both MODE and ACCTY continue to play approximately the same role for both cities. This could mean that they do in fact play the role as prescribed by their respective coefficients or that they are both misspecified to the same degree in both cities. The truth is probably someplace in between. Nonetheless, it is gratifying to see the very small statistical difference that exists between the two cities for these variables particularly in terms of their positive signs.

The R^2 for Milwaukee of (.37) for equation (2) was considerably better than that for Buffalo (R^2 of .23), which is also reflected in their *F*-tests (69.4 for Milwaukee versus 35.8 for Buffalo). The standard deviation was also reduced somewhat (1.37 versus 1.43) but not as much as one would like (i.e., some number less than one since both cities are quite compact).

Equation (3) presents no real surprises either. CH is less important both numerically (.00017 versus .00040) and statistically ("t" test of 3.37 versus 4.91) for Milwaukee than Buffalo but the difference is still not very great. The differences between the coefficients for both LOCH and SZF are about .02, with Buffalo being numerically higher than Milwaukee. In short, there is not much real difference between the empirical results for the two cities for equation (3). This is all the more remarkable in view of the fact that the R^2 for both is between .16 and .17, which indicates there is a lot left to be explained—that is, in view of such a low R^2, it seems that it would be quite possible for these three variables to play a significantly different role in both cities.

The low R^2 and the relatively high standard deviation of approximately .66 indicate that it is very difficult to explain housing type with such a simplified, linear, economic type approach.

Summarizing the Comparison

Remarkably enough, there do not appear to be any major statistical or numerical differences existing for this model as yielded by the data from Buffalo and Milwaukee. The most important aspect of this comparison is the signs on the variables that were completely consistent. The next important dimension was the statistical results that did reveal some differences. The major ones are (a) the change in the roles of YN and RACE in equation (2) between Milwaukee and Buffalo; and (b) the higher explanatory power of equation (2) for Milwaukee over Buffalo.

The final dimension is the differences in the numerical results or the constants and coefficients of which the major ones are (a) the complete reversal of the constant in equation (1) from a highly positive number to a slightly negative one; and (b) the decreased numerical importance of RACE and the overall increased importance of YN for Milwaukee versus Buffalo in equation (2).

Thus, it appears that the functional form of this model as presented in Chapter Four, which was used in the Buffalo analysis, can also be validly used to analyze residential location in Milwaukee.

SIMULATIONS WITH THE MILWAUKEE MODEL

Simulation 1: Simple Run

The first simulation takes the Milwaukee regression model (Table 6–2) and then compares the allocation results by number of households per ring and sector and by housing type with the original allocations (note Figure 6–1 for a map depicting Milwaukee's rings and sectors).

Table 6–4 presents the allocation results for the number of households allocated per ring and sector. For example, the original allocation for ring 1, sector 1 was 33 households, but the Milwaukee regression model allocates

Figure 6–1. Map of Milwaukee—Rings and Sectors.

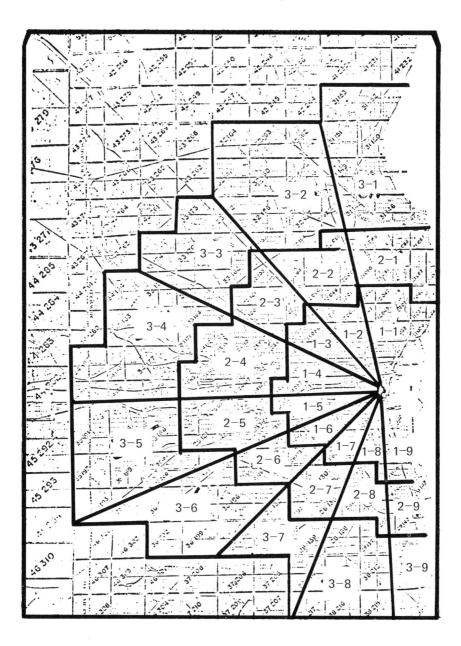

Table 6–4. Simulation 1: Simple Run, Milwaukee

Ring	Sector	Original Allocation	Model Allocation
1	1	33	19
1	2	22	24
1	3	27	8
1	4	14	1
1	5	18	1
1	6	20	1
1	7	20	2
1	8	19	1
1	9	12 (185)	5 (62)
			(54B–8W)
2	1	22	21
2	2	22	28
2	3	22	29
2	4	22	27
2	5	22	29
2	6	22	24
2	7	22	32
2	8	22	37
2	9	22 (198)	27 (254)
3	1	22	37
3	2	22	14
3	3	22	34
3	4	22	30
3	5	22	32
3	6	22	39
3	7	22	30
3	8	22	25
3	9	22 (198)	24 (265)

Note: Totals per ring are in parentheses.

only 19 households to ring 1, sector 1, which is a net loss of 14 households. The major results of the first simulation are as follows. First, ring 1 (including all sectors) is effectively inhabited only by non-white families—that is, of the 62 families living in ring 1, 54 are non-white. These non-white families also originally inhabited ring 1 (mostly in sectors 1 and 2), which implies that they remain stationary. Thus, the Milwaukee regression model results may be interpreted to predict that the central city will eventually be inhabited only by non-whites. Second, the remaining 123 families from ring 1 are reallocated to ring 2, which gains (net) 56 families. This implies a fairly significant increase in density for the outer areas of the city. The reason that ring 2 does not increase even more in density is that many of ring 2's original allocation of households is reallocated to ring 3. Third, ring 3 gains 67 households over its original allocation, which is due to the migration of ring 2's original residents from the outer areas of the city to the proximate suburbs. The area in the suburbs that had the highest net gain was that closest to the city boundary. This would imply the new construction of two-family and multi-family structures (on vacant lands and land formerly occupied by single-family residences) to house the higher densities. Such construction patterns run contrary to the previous ones for these areas, which formerly emphasized single-family construction.

Housing Type. Table 6–5 indicates what the model predicts in terms of housing type inhabited. For ring 1, 11 households inhabit single-family residences, which is approximately 18 percent of the total households versus 43 percent in the original allocation (11:79 versus 61:185). For two-family residences, the model predicts that 60 percent will inhabit these units versus 52 percent for the original data. Multi-family units retain approximately the same level of importance with the model predicting a 23 percent rate, while the original rate was 21 percent. Thus, the model reallocates families from single-family residences to two-family structures. This does not make much sense if ring 1's population declined in absolute (or relative) terms to the degree the model indicates (i.e., 61 families versus 185 families) but does make some sense if it is remembered that increases in center city population often come from in-migrants (which the model does not include as it deals with a fixed population) who may be forced to increasingly live in higher density housing due to the more rapid deterioration of single-family units (i.e., for some central city areas, single-family units are the oldest ones). It may also occur if the rate of influx of in-migrants exceeds the rate at which the ghetto expands.

For ring 2, there is a modest decline in the importance of single-family residences from 43 percent to 39 percent (85:101 versus 198:254). The direction would certainly appear to be correct, given an increase in density of approximately 28 percent, but the magnitude is probably understated by a considerable amount. Two-family structures increase in importance from 45 percent to 52 percent. Once again, the direction is probably correct, but the magnitude may be understated. For multi-family residences, the relative importance declines from 12 percent to 9 percent. This result is wrong both directionally and magnitudinally as it is this type of housing whose importance would most dramatically increase due to the increase in population density. Consequently, the model fails in its analysis of the change in housing structure inhabited for ring 2.

For ring 3, the Milwaukee regression model increases the importance of single-family residences from 77 percent to 84 percent (154:223 versus 198:265), which is probably incorrect directionally and magnitudinally—that is, if ring 3 (the first ring of suburbs or the more mature suburbs) experiences an increase in population of approximately 34 percent, this would probably entail a net reduction in the relative importance of single-family residences as much of the increase would be housed in more dense housing such as two-family and (particularly) multi-family housing. This will be modified to the extent that there are large vacant areas in ring 3, which could accommodate large increases in population via single-family residences. However, this modification does not

Table 6–5. Simulation 1: Simple Run, Allocation of Households, by Household Type, Milwaukee

Ring	Sector	Single-Family		Two-Family		Multi-Family	
		Original Data Allocation	Model Allocation	Original Data Allocation	Model Allocation	Original Data Allocation	Model Allocation
1	1	7	3	9	10	17	6
1	2	6	7	12	14	4	3
1	3	18	1	19	5	0	2
1	4	0	0	4	1	10	0
1	5	15	0	2	1	1	0
1	6	14	0	6	1	0	0
1	7	4	0	15	1	1	1
1	8	9	0	8	0	2	1
1	9	16 (79)	0 (11)	2 (97)	4 (37)	4 (39)	1 (14)
2	1	7	7	10	12	5	2
2	2	10	11	9	15	3	2
2	3	6	13	14	14	2	2
2	4	8	9	12	14	2	3
2	5	11	10	9	15	2	4
2	6	12	11	8	11	2	2
2	7	9	12	10	16	3	4
2	8	9	16	12	18	1	3
2	9	13 (85)	13 (101)	6 (90)	13 (129)	3 (23)	2 (24)
3	1	18	30	1	7	3	0
3	2	13	12	4	2	5	0
3	3	15	28	5	6	2	0
3	4	22	28	0	2	0	0
3	5	16	27	4	5	2	0
3	6	19	31	3	8	0	0
3	7	20	25	1	5	1	0
3	8	13	20	4	5	5	0
3	9	18 (154)	22 (223)	2 (24)	2 (52)	2 (20)	0 (0)

Note: Totals per ring by housing type are in parentheses.

seem likely to be the case since ring 3 does contain the older suburbs, which are probably built-up to a large degree.

Two-family residences increase in importance from 12 percent to 16 percent, which is probably accurate in terms of direction but may be an understatement magnitudinally due to the large increase in population for ring 3. Multi-family units are not present at all with the regression results (versus 11 percent for the original data), which is clearly a serious failure on the part of the regression model—that is, much of the increase in population would probably have to be housed in multi-family structures. The failure of the regression model to at least replicate the percentage figure for the original data reflects the low R^2 of equation (3), which allocates households by housing type. If the regression model's performance is to be improved, this equation will have to be restructured using variables (not yet available or generated) that more accurately explain choice of housing type.

Another aspect of this particular problem of analyzing housing type is that the regression model is really only analyzing quantities demanded. The introduction of a meaningful supply function (not simply a linear constraint that was employed in the previous chapter), which would be sensitive to changes in relative prices, costs, and so forth, would produce an equilibrium allocation that would undoubtedly reflect a large increase in the number of multi-family units inhabited. It would accomplish this by reflecting the fact that as population increases, the demand for single- and two-family homes would rise to the extent that their equilibrium price (assuming a stable supply curve due to rise in land costs equaling productivity increase in residential construction) would exceed the budget constraint for housing of many families. If, as seems likely, land price increases exceed residential construction productivity, increases housing prices will rise even faster as the supply curve shifts to the left. Thus, if people are to be housed within the limits of their budget, the higher price (particularly of land) must be spread over more units, which necessitates the construction of multi-family units.

F-Test for LOCH and TYPR. The analysis of variance performed with regard to this simulation is analagous to those tests performed on the Buffalo model's simulations in which one tests whether the simulation allocation results are significantly different from the original data allocations and/or some other simulations allocation results. Basically, this is done by comparing variances about the means of the two different allocations (or distributions). In this particular instance, the results of the simple data run via the regression model are compared with the original data allocations. The results are presented in Table 6-6.

For LOCH (linear distance of the residence from the CBD), the *F*-test yielded a value of 4.0038. This is significant at the .05 level, which implies that the residential allocation patterns yielded by the regression model are

Table 6–6.   Simulation 1: F-Test for LOCH and TYPR, Milwaukee

Variable	Source of Variation		Sum of Squares	Degrees of Freedom	Mean Square
LOCH	BETWEEN RESULTS		3.6418	1	3.6418
TYPR			.2596	1	.2592
LOCH	ERROR		1055.1360	1160	.9096
TYPR			219.2400	1160	.1890
LOCH			1058.7778	1161	
TYPR		TOTAL	219.4996	1161	

F of LOCH   =   4.0038
F of TYPR   =   1.3713
$F_{.05}$ (1,1160) = 3.84[a]

a. Samuel Richmond, *Statistical Analysis* (Ronald Press, New York, 1965), p. 580.

significantly different than those yielded by their original allocation. This is not too surprising in view of (a) the numerical results presented in Table 6–4; and (b) the R^2 of equation (2) of .37 and the R^2 of .74 of equation (1), which feeds into equation (2).

The F-test on TYPR yields a value of 1.3713, which is insignificant, which implies that the housing types yielded by the regression model are not significantly different than those present in the original data. This is surprising in view of (a) the R^2 of equation (1) of .74, which feeds into equation (2) with an R^2 of .37, both of which then feed into equation (3); (b) equation (3) itself has an R^2 of only .16; (c) the percentage changes in the types of housing (inhibited) as yielded by the regression model versus those percentages that existed in the original data (e.g., single-family homes accounted for 50 percent of the total in the original data and 55.5 percent in the regression model's results; two-family housing was 36 percent of the total with the original data and 38 percent with the regression models results; and finally multi-family housing accounted for 14 percent of the total in the original data and only 6.5 percent with the regression models results).

A possible explanation is that (as stated in Chapter Five) the regression model produces a fairly continuous distribution for TYPR (e.g., 1.213, 1.216, . . . 2.220, 2.223 . . . etc.), which when compared with the actual discrete data of 1s, 2s and 3s may grossly understate the differences particularly when the test is one involving means. To correct for this, the regression distribution for TYPR which was amended to be discrete (i.e., if TYPR = 1.4, TYPR was set equal to one), was compared with the discrete original data, which yielded an F-value of 5.213, which is significant at the .05 level. To the extent that this latter procedure is more correct, one can state that the regression values for TYPR are significantly different than the original data for TYPR.

Supply Constraint. Although a linear, descriptive supply constraint was used in conjunction with the Buffalo model, its major effect was to allocate households more evenly (vis-à-vis the regression models' allocations) such that the equilibrium allocations more closely approximated the original data allocations. However, this constraint, by its very nature, did not reflect true economic or market phenomenon in that it too failed to produce the necessary amount of multi-family dwellings that were implied by the regression model's allocations. This was due to the non-functional (i.e., did not contain economically causal variables that reflected changes in market conditions such as relative prices and costs) and non-dynamic nature of the supply function. Consequently, due to its mediocre performance, such a supply constraint was not used in conjunction with the Milwaukee regression model. The ideal supply function was not constructed and implemented due to the unavailability of data.

Simulation 2: Increased Income
for Blacks versus Open Occupancy

The purpose of this simulation is to determine whether increased income or open occupancy would be more effective in breaking up the ghetto. To the extent that blacks are charged significantly higher rents than whites for comparable housing because the ghetto population is rising faster than the ghetto is expanding (or blacks dispersing themselves without open occupancy), open occupancy may be the most effective policy because it allows blacks to bid for housing anywhere they desire. Since they are paying higher rents than whites for comparable housing, they should be able to bid some housing away from whites (or cause new housing not in the ghetto to be produced for them) and remove themselves from the ghetto. If, however, a ghetto exists because the residents can only afford cheaper housing (assuming here that whites and blacks spend approximately the same for comparable housing) due to insufficient income, then the problem of dispersing the ghetto becomes one of increasing ghetto incomes. The second alternative does this by increasing blacks income by $1,000 per annum.

A methodological problem arises (as discussed at length in the previous chapter) as to which regression model to use to simulate blacks' behavior. Should it be the entire regression model, which includes 61 black families and 520 white families, or a regression model containing only black families. Using the entire samples (581) regression model implies that blacks, when constraints are removed, will modify their behavior to act more in accordance with white families who do not face these constraints. This behavioral assumption would particularly apply to the open-occupancy simulation. One could also assume that as one's income rises, one emulates the behavior of those in the higher income class with some ratchet effect. This would apply to the simulation that increases black's income.

Using the regression results based on the data for "blacks only" implies that they will not greatly change their behavior as constraints are removed or as they increase their incomes. The regression results for blacks only (61 families) is presented in Table 6–7, which are dramatically different than those for the entire sample of 581 (Table 6–2). For example, in equation (1), the constant for the entire sample was −64.02, whereas for blacks it is 419.74. In conjunction with this, the coefficient on Y goes down from .14 for the entire sample to .10 for blacks. Taken together, using only the constant and Y, a black family with an income of $7,000 would spend $1,119.75 on housing per annum using the blacks regression results and $916.00 using the entire samples results or a difference of $200 or 22 percent. The YN variable changes sign from a positive .057 to a negative −.003, but this can be attributed to multi-collinearity between YN and OCCUP (r of .05 between YN and CH and r of .20 between YN and OCCUP) as shown in Table 6–8. More importantly, YN is not significant, which may imply that income class clustering does not occur to a very great extent in the ghetto, which in turn may be related to the constraints placed on the mobility of blacks. OCCUP has a positive sign in both cases but is insignificant in the "blacks only" case. In short, the "blacks only" results indicate that what is spent on housing is a function of Y only (r of .92; see Table 6–8) and that there is a very high and significant intercept. Together they give some credence to the assertion that blacks do spend more for comparable housing than do whites with the percentage difference declining with rises in income. This economic or cost effect of segregation has been found to exist, using census data, in 30 major cities in the United States.[2] The implication of these findings is that open occupancy is a potentially effective policy for breaking up the ghetto.

The second equation is almost completely different with the only similarity being the MODE variable, which has a positive sign in both cases and is

Table 6–7. Simulation 2: Regression Results for Blacks Only, Milwaukee

(1)   CH = 419.740 + .1016 Y − .0037 YN + 46.22 OCCUP
          (166.72)   (.0055)   (.0315)   (34.32)

Standard Deviation = 123.945 R^2 = .8523

(2)   LOCH = − 1.018 − .00013 CH + .00045 YN + .8783 RACE
              (.7235) (.00016)   (.00011)   (.221)

          + .2516 MODE − .005 ACCTY
            (.1044)   (.0034)

(3)   TYPR = 2.399 + .00019 CH − .0128 LOCH − .1497 SZF
              (.5123) (.00025)   (.1852)   (.0370)

Standard Deviation = .6526 R^2 = .1735

Table 6–8. Simulation 2: Correlation Matrix for Blacks Only, Milwaukee

	RACE	AGE	OCCUP	MODE	LOCH	LOCW	PCAR	Y	YN	CH	TYPR	SZF
AGE	0.16											
MODE	0.12	-0.27										
OCCUP	-0.24	0.03		0.18								
LOCH	0.14	0.07	0.03	0.17								
LOCW	0.27	0.26	0.17	0.37	-0.10							
PCAR	-0.09	-0.08	-0.11	0.18	0.03	-0.08						
Y	-0.06	-0.22	-0.12	0.15	-0.05	-0.12	0.24					
YN	-0.53	-0.24	0.36	0.18	0.31	-0.27	0.15	0.07				
CH	-0.00	-0.21	0.20	0.20	-0.09	-0.04	0.29	0.92	0.05			
TYPR	-0.33	0.14	0.28	0.00	-0.01	-0.15	-0.09	0.11	-0.08	0.04		
SZF	0.25	-0.22	-0.11	0.22	-0.04	0.22	0.16	-0.04	-0.18	0.11	-0.45	
ACCTY	0.27	0.13	0.04	0.22	-0.12	0.87	0.03	0.29	-0.20	0.37	-0.13	0.26

also significant for both. CH is not significant, which may reinforce the findings for YN in equation (1) in that the amount spent on housing does not have much effect on where one lives in the ghetto. YN is significant here, which this author cannot really explain. Race is significant but cannot be seen as playing much of a role since effectively all residents in the ghetto are black. ACCTY has a negative sign (and r is also $-.12$) but is not significant. If it were, it would imply that blacks work further out from the CBD than where they live (also note r of $-.10$ between LOCH and LOCW), which is normally not held to be the case (i.e., blacks are supposed to live in close proximity to their jobs, most of which are in or near the CBD or in the ghetto itself).

Equation (3) is also fraught with dramatic contrasts. CH has a positive sign and is insignificant in the "blacks only" regression results, which correspond with previous comments about the unpredictability surrounding housing expenditures as related to location. It may also be a result of the housing stock itself—that is, given the age distribution of general conditions of the housing stock in the ghetto, it is not clear that single-family residences would cost more or be an improvement over two-family or multi-family residences. LOCH has the correct sign but is insignificant (note: r of $-.01$ between LOCH and TYPR), which may also be a reflection of a more random distribution of housing in the ghetto. SZF has the correct sign and is significant, which indicates that blacks as well as whites seek more housing, "ceteris paribus," as their families grow.

As with the Buffalo simulation, this author feels it is more valid to use the entire samples' model results with all that implies about behavior. A further reason involves the difficulty of re-estimating an entirely new model and examining its implications for this simulation particularly with respect to the RACE variable, which has no real content or meaning when used with black household data only.

Simulation Methodology. The two simulations via the regression model were accomplished as follows: (1) to simulate an increase of $1,000 per annum in income, for blacks, the Y variable in the first equation was raised by $1,000 for blacks with the coefficients remaining the same in all equations. The data for black families was then run through the model with this increase for blacks included. The results in terms of allocation and housing type are shown in Tables 6–9, and 6–10, respectively.

To simulate the policy of completely effective open occupancy, the coefficient on the RACE variable was changed from -1.0 to 0. The data for black families was then run through the model with this change (i.e., this change effects only LOCH and TYPR directly). This serves only to analyze the potential effects of open occupancy because it does not account for those blacks who could move (i.e., afford to economically) but would not because they would choose to continue to live within the confines of the ghetto.

Table 6–9. Simulation 2: Increased Income for Blacks versus Open Occupancy, Allocation of Households, Milwaukee

Ring	Sector	Original	Model	Income Increased by $1,000	Open Occupancy
1	1	19	19	16	3
1	2	22	23	22	5
1	3	7	7	7	3
1	7	3	1	0	0
1	9	5 (55)	4 (54)	1 (46)	0 (11)
2	1	0	1	3	19
2	2	6	4	6	21
2	3	0	0	0	4
2	7	0	2	3	1
2	9	0 (6)	0 (7)	1 (13)	3 (48)
3	1	0	0	0	0
3	2	0	0	2	0
3	3	0	0	0	0
3	7	0	0	0	2
3	9	0 (0)	0 (0)	0 (2)	0 (2)
		61	61	61	61

Note: Totals per ring are in parentheses.

Allocation Results of Simulation 2. Table 6–9 indicates the extent to which blacks could increase their consumption of housing as a result of increased income or open occupancy. However, certain limitations should be noted. It is fairly obvious that if one increases income vis-à-vis the regression model CH rises, which together with its negative coefficient in equation (3), causes a move toward single-family living or a reduction in living densities. A priori, it does not seem that an open-occupancy policy would simultaneously enable a family to move (a major effect) and decrease its living density because nominal income has not changed. However, real income can go up as a result of open occupancy if the black family was formerly paying more for comparable housing than a white family was paying. Open occupancy then allows him to bid against whites at lower prices (or rents) than he would be facing in the ghetto. The greater is the factor of segregation and the more it leads to higher rents (not the same thing), the more effective is open occupancy in raising real incomes for blacks. One could even conceive of a situation where open occupancy could approach our income subsidy in its effects on real income.

The results of the two simulations on housing type (Table 6–10) indicate that the increase in income will allow 12 more families to inhabit single-family residences than previously was the case. This is a dramatic increase of 63 percent. All of the 12 had previously inhabited two-family structures.

Table 6–10. Simulation 2: Increased Income for Blacks versus Open Occupancy, Allocation by Housing Type, Milwaukee

Ring	Sector	Original			Model			Income Increased by $1,000			Open Occupancy		
		Housing Type											
		1	2	3	1	2	3	1	2	3	1	2	3
1	1	2	11	9	4	10	5	6	7	3	1	2	0
1	2	7	10	2	7	14	3	12	7	3	2	1	2
1	3	2	5	0	1	5	1	2	4	1	3	0	0
1	7	1	2	0	0	0	1	0	0	0	0	0	0
1	9	3	1	0	0	3	1	0	1	0	0	0	0
2	1	0	0	0	0	1	0	2	1	0	10	8	1
2	2	4	2	0	2	2	0	5	1	0	15	4	2
2	3	0	0	0	0	0	0	0	0	0	2	2	0
2	7	0	0	0	2	0	0	2	1	0	0	1	0
2	9	0	0	0	0	0	0	2	1	0	2	1	0
3	1	0	0	0	0	0	0	0	0	0	0	0	0
3	2	0	0	0	0	0	0	0	0	0	0	0	0
3	3	0	0	0	0	0	0	0	0	0	0	0	0
3	7	0	0	0	0	0	0	0	0	0	2	0	0
3	9	0	0	0	0	0	0	0	0	0	0	0	0
		19	31	11	16	34	11	31	23	7	37	19	5

Note: Type 1 = Single-Family Residences.
        Type 2 = Two-Family Residences.
        Type 3 = Multi-Family Residences.

There were also 4 families who moved from multi-family residences to two-family residences (i.e., a reduction in multi-family residences of 36 percent).

The open-occupancy policy allowed 18 families (increase of 95 percent) to move from two-family residences to single-family residences. Further, 6 families were able to move from multi-family residences to two-family residences or a net reduction of 55 percent in multi-family residences inhabited.

Thus open occupancy is the most effective policy both in terms of dispersing the ghetto and improving the density of housing inhabited. This is because segregation has produced the potential for economic conditions (namely, quantities demanded exceeding quantities supplied for housing to a greater extent for blacks than whites), which have led blacks to spend so much more for comparable housing than do whites that open occupancy allows them to increase their real incomes and hence disperse more widely and effectively than does a $1,000 increase in income. Of course, this is restricted to the housing market only. It may well be that the total utility for some will be greater under the income plan depending on whether their increase in real income as a result of open occupancy exceeds the utility from the $1,000 subsidy or grant.

There are certain other modifications that should be examined to better determine what the actual equilibrium effect of these two policies would be—that is, these simulations reflected what would be demanded by the households effected, not what their final equilibrium allocations would be. For this, we need to introduce the necessary supply function(s) and examine their interaction to determine what the final equilibrium prices and quantities would be. Consequently, the two simulations that reflect desires or housing quantities demanded probably overstate the final effect particularly with regard to TYPR or housing density because as the black families seek housing outside the ghetto, effective demand for housing will rise and thus (given a stable supply curve that seems reasonable since increases in land costs will probably offset any increases in residential construction productivity) produce a higher price (or rent), which means that families' desires will not be met at the previous level of prices.

Further, if those who receive the increased income attempt to move out of the ghetto, they may not be able to without some form of an open-occupancy policy. The final effect with such a policy might well be a bidding up of rents within the ghetto as the black residents all scramble for better housing. The ultimate benefactor in this instance would be some (if not all) the owners of rental property within the ghetto. A possible objection to this conclusion is that it could be noted that it is irrational for property owners outside the ghetto to refuse to do business with black households particularly in view of their increased spending power. Consequently, as blacks experience increased incomes, they will be able to leave the ghetto and improve the housing they consume. It is difficult to judge whether property entrepreneurs are economically irrational if they discriminate in their rental and/or selling activities. The fact of the matter is that they do (the Supreme Court notwithstanding) and the results are those that have previously been discussed.

The extent to which black residents raise their real incomes via open occupancy (note: all blacks should benefit from such a policy whether they actually are the ones who move or not because of the net reduction in demand for ghetto housing) will also be limited by the equilibrium price being higher than that now prevailing in the white areas due to increased demand for this housing (i.e., those blacks who now bid for it who could not before). The overall effect should be a smoothing of the rent gradient for comparable housing between the black and white areas. However, to the extent that higher rents in the black areas are a result of higher costs incurred by the housing entrepreneurs to service this housing, rents for blacks (within the ghetto) for comparable housing will be higher and remain higher. With this set of data, it is not possible to determine how much of the 20 to 30 percent rent differential is due to higher costs of service and how much occurs as a result of housing segregation. It is probably safe to assume that both play a substantial role.

Open occupancy will allow certain low service cost families to move out of the ghetto and live with other families that incur the same level of service costs (particularly if they are now unable to do this because of the severely constrained available supply of housing, which restricts their alternatives and mobility) so that they are not forced to assume the burden of others' costs in a disproportionate manner. As this occurs, it will become apparent how much of the rent differential was due to segregation and how much to higher service costs.

F-Test for LOCH and TYPR. Table 6–11 presents the analysis of variance for the variables LOCH and TYPR as they were generated by the two policy simulations. That is, the *F*-test determines whether the two simulations produced results for LOCH and TYPR that were significantly different from each other (note: they were not compared with the original allocations). The results for both are significant at the .05 level (*F* for LOCH is 41.74 and for TYPR is 4.67) with LOCH being significant at the .01 level also. Thus, we can say that the two simulations did produce results that were significantly (at the .05 level) different from each other.

Simulation 3: Change in Work
Accessibility to Ring 1

The object of this simulation was to test what the effect of a change in accessibility to work would be on residential location. The simulation changed the accessibility to work for those employed in ring 1 by halving the commuting distance (time) to work. Mechanically, this was performed by halving the LOCW

Table 6–11.   Simulation 2: Increased Income for Blacks versus Open Occupancy, Milwaukee

F-Test for LOCH and TYPR
Statistics for One Way Analysis of Variance

Variable	Source of Variation	Sum of Squares	Degrees of Freedom	Mean Square
LOCH	BETWEEN RESULTS	2.6977	1	2.6977
TYPR		.0152	1	.0152
LOCH		7.7520	120	.0646
TYPR	ERROR	.0960	120	.0032
LOCH	TOTAL	10.4497	121	
TYPR		.1112	121	

F(1,120) LOCH = 41.7358
F(1,120) TYPR = 4.6733
$F_{.05}$ (1,120) = 3.92[a]

a. Samuel Richmond, *Statistical Analysis*, p. 579.

component of the accessibility variable ACCTY (i.e., ACCTY = LOCW * Y). The data were then run through the model using the coefficients based on the entire areas data (Table 6–2).

Theoretically, one would expect that by reducing this element of the cost of accessibility so dramatically, the distribution of households would spread out—that is, there would be "ceteris paribus," a general outward movement of households for those employed in the center city from ring 1 to ring 2, from ring 2 to ring 3, and so forth. In other words, if the price of commuting is reduced, households will substitute some distance for it (substitution effect) by moving further out and probably buy more housing (income effect) as well.

However, contrary to this, an examination of Table 6–12 reveals just the opposite. To begin with, there is a net movement of 4 percent (22:581) of the households that are relocated, whereas 40 percent of the households are potentially affected (i.e., the head of the household works in ring 1). This seems

Table 6–12. Simulation 3: Change in Work Accessibility to Ring 1, Milwaukee

Ring	Sector	Original Data	Model Allocation	Accessibility Change Allocation
1	1	33	19	19
1	2	22	24	24
1	3	27	8	8
1	4	14	1	1
1	5	18	1	1
1	6	20	1	1
1	7	20	2	2
1	8	19	1	1
1	9	12 (185)	5 (62)	5 (62)
2	1	22	21	19
2	2	22	28	32
2	3	22	29	32
2	4	22	27	25
2	5	22	29	31
2	6	22	32	28
2	7	22	37	35
2	8	22	27	39
2	9	22 (198)	(254)	30 (276)
3	1	22	37	38
3	2	22	14	9
3	3	22	34	30
3	4	22	30	31
3	5	22	32	30
3	6	22	39	35
3	7	22	30	27
3	8	22	25	23
3	9	22 (198)	24 (265)	20 (243)

to reflect earlier statements about the minor (and perhaps understated) role that linear distance (time) to work plays in determining residential location.

More surprising is the direction of household movement predicted, which is not outward but rather inward (i.e., from ring 3 to ring 2). This is due to the positive correlation between LOCH and LOCW (Table 6–13), which implies that the further out one's workplace, the further out one lives. Given this factor, the problem in direction predicted must lie with the substitution of distance for time in the accessibility variable. This was justified earlier on the grounds of their high correlation (i.e., $R^2 > .9$). This too is acceptable if we assume a static transportation network. The use of distance as a proxy breaks down though when the static situation is altered drastically and continues to fail until the system returns to its former equilibrium state. For example, if a new freeway is constructed increasing accessibility to the center city from the outer areas of the city, households will begin to locate in the outer areas until the freeway becomes so congested that time and distance once again become highly correlated (particularly at rush hour periods when most work trips are made). At this point, it is no longer advantageous to locate in the outer fringes because the price or cost of accessibility is effectively equal at all points in the area. There will be no further income and substitution effects via this particular change in the transport network.

In short, the model has failed to depict the disequilibrium adjustment movements that would occur in bringing the residential location situation back to equilibrium, which would entail a net household movement outward rather than inward. This failure can further be attributed to the fact that this is basically a comparative statics model rather than a dynamic model.

Interestingly enough, the simulation (Table 6–14) does seem to reflect a slight real income effect (due to price or cost of accessibility falling), with single family housing being slightly more important proportionally in both rings 2 and 3 when compared with the "model allocations."

Analysis of Variance for Variables LOCH and TYPR.   The results of the analysis of variance for LOCH and TYPR for the simulation 3's allocations versus the "models allocations" are shown in Table 6–15. The relatively minor changes (less than 5 percent of the total) for both variables are reflected in the fact that the F-tests for both are insignificant (i.e., F of .0416 for LOCH and F of .0074 for TYPR). This analysis of variance indicates that the allocation results produced by simulation three and by the model for these two variables are not significantly different, or in other words, do not represent two different simulations.

Table 6–13.   Simulation 3: Correlation Matrix for Milwaukee Data

	RACE	AGE	MODE	OCCUP	LOCH	LOCW	PCAR	Y	YN	CH	TYPR	SZF
AGE	-0.14											
MODE	-0.08	0.15										
OCCUP	-0.12	-0.06	0.20									
LOCH	-0.35	0.14	0.15	0.21								
LOCW	-0.01	-0.01	0.10	0.23	0.13							
PCAR	-0.14	0.07	0.08	0.38	0.28	0.14						
Y	-0.12	0.16	0.23	0.19	0.33	-0.00	0.45					
YN	-0.33	0.18	0.19	0.14	0.54	-0.02	0.25	0.40				
CH	-0.20	0.21	0.20	0.18	0.44	0.01	0.39	0.84	0.50			
TYPR	0.15	-0.22	-0.12	-0.11	-0.31	-0.10	-0.31	-0.22	-0.24	-0.27		
SZF	0.06	-0.21	-0.05	0.11	-0.02	0.15	0.20	0.08	-0.03	0.05	-0.22	
ACCTY	-0.07	0.07	0.17	0.25	0.24	0.82	0.32	0.42	0.14	0.36	-0.20	0.15

Table 6–14.   Simulation 3: Change in Accessibility to Ring 1, Allocation of Households, by Household Type, Milwaukee

		Single-Family			Two-Family			Multi-Family		
Ring	Sector	Original Data	Model	Accessibility Change	Original Data	Model	Accessibility Change	Original Data	Model	Accessibility Change
1	1	7	3	3	9	10	10	17	6	6
1	2	6	7	7	12	14	14	4	3	3
1	3	18	1	1	19	5	5	0	2	2
1	4	0	0	0	4	1	1	10	0	0
1	5	15	0	0	2	1	1	1	0	0
1	6	14	0	0	6	1	1	0	1	1
1	7	4	0	0	15	1	1	1	1	1
1	8	9	0	0	8	0	0	2	1	1
1	9	16 (79)	0 (11)	0 (11)	2 (97)	4 (37)	0 (37)	4 (39)	1 (14)	1 (14)
2	1	7	7	7	10	12	11	5	2	2
2	2	10	11	11	9	15	20	3	2	2
2	3	6	13	14	14	14	17	2	3	4
2	4	8	9	9	12	14	13	2	4	3
2	5	11	10	13	9	15	13	2	2	5
2	6	12	11	11	8	11	14	3	4	3
2	7	9	12	15	10	16	16	1	3	4
2	8	9	16	18	12	18	18	3	2	3
2	9	13 (85)	12 (101)	14 (112)	6 (90)	13 (129)	14 (136)	3 (23)	2 (24)	2 (28)
3	1	18	30	30	1	7	8	3	0	0
3	2	13	12	8	4	2	1	5	0	0
3	3	15	28	25	5	6	5	2	0	0
3	4	22	28	29	0	2	2	0	0	0
3	5	16	27	27	4	5	3	2	0	0
3	6	19	31	29	3	8	6	1	0	0
3	7	20	25	24	1	5	3	5	0	0
3	8	13	20	21	4	5	2	5	0	0
3	9	18 (154)	22 (223)	19 (212)	2 (24)	2 (42)	1 (31)	2 (20)	0 (0)	0 (0)

Table 6–15. Simulation 3: Accessibility Change, Analysis of Variance for LOCH and TYPR between Model Results and Simulation Results, Milwaukee

Variable	Source of Variation	Sum of Squares	Degree of Freedom	Mean Square
LOCH	BETWEEN RESULTS	.0432	1	.0432
TYPR		.0005	1	.0005
LOCH		1202.8	1160	1.0369
	ERROR			
TYPR		75.284	1160	.0649
LOCH	TOTAL	1202.8432	1161	
TYPR		75.2845	1161	

F(LOCH) = .0416
F(TYPR) = .0074

Simulation 4: Comparing Allocational Effects of Using a Regression Model Based on Data from Rings 1 and 2 (City Only) versus a Model Based on Data from Ring 3 (Suburbs)

The purpose of this simulation is to determine whether the locational and housing preferences of suburban dwellers are a simple projection of those of city dwellers—that is, are suburbanites merely wealthier city dwellers who can afford single-family homes more readily. Are there also city dwellers who choose to live farther from work because they prefer space to proximity to work or are the differences more profound? The answer to these questions can be answered by first examining the results of two different sets of regression coefficients, with one set based on the data for the city (rings 1 and 2) dwellers and the other data for suburbanites (ring 3); and secondly by examining the difference in the allocational effects of the two sets of regression coefficients.

The Regression Results Compared. Table 6–16 presents the regression results for rings 1 and 2 (city only) with Table 6–17 presenting the correlation matrix for this data. In comparing the results for this data with the data for the whole area (rings 1, 2, and 3), equation (1) is essentially the same in both with the only difference being a lower R^2 with the "city only" data (i.e., R^2 of .52 for city only data as R^2 of .74 for the whole area's data).

Equation (2) presents only one surprise, which is the positive sign on the RACE variable. This is due to multi-collinearity problems with the Y variable—that is, the r between RACE and LOCH is −.34 (correct sign in terms of indicating segregation and in agreement with negative sign with model results for all the data) whereas the r between RACE and YN is −.58.

Table 6–16.   Simulation 4: Regression Results for Rings 1 and 2, OLS, Milwaukee

(1)   CH   = − 121.44635 + .11549 Y + .08825 YN + 36.499240 OCCUP
            (120.10289)   (.00643)   (.018937)   (36.12806)

   Standard Deviation = 346.2949 $R^2 = .5173$

(2)   LOCH = − 1.50346 + .00014 CH + .00064 YN + .12342 RACE
              (.31510)   (.00008)   (.00005)   (.12333)

       + .017255 MODE + .00291 ACCTY
          (.082196)   (.00165)

   Standard Deviation = .72158 $R^2 = .4304$

(3)   TYPR = 2.51980 − .00012 CH − .07893 LOCH − .10717 SZF
              (.14386)   (.00007)   (.03821)   (.01927)

   Standard Deviation = .67703 $R^2 = .0901$

   Equation (3) is also essentially the same as that for the model containing all the data. In short, the regression results using the data for rings 1 and 2 are almost completely analogous (particularly in terms of the signs on the coefficients) to those results obtained when all the data (rings 1, 2, and 3) is employed.

   Table 6–18 and 6–19 present the regression and correlation matrix findings respectively for the data for ring 3 (suburbs only). The results for equation (1) for ring 3 and for the model using all the data are quite comparable.[a] The major difference is the more dominant role played by the Y variable (t-value of 32.9 for all the data and 17.9 for rings 1 and 2, and t-value of 81.0 for data of ring 3) in the results for ring 3. This also leads to a much higher R^2 of .98 for ring 3 versus R^2 of .74 for all the data. Thus, the view that suburbanites are simply richer city dwellers with income being the dominant variable in separating the two may be partially borne out by this equation.

   Equation (2) is dramatically different for the two sets of data. To begin with, only one variable, ACCTY is significant in the results for ring 3. This result becomes more apparent when the correlation matrix in Table 6–19 is examined. It indicates that there are no important variables appearing that are not already included (note: CH is present instead of Y and ACCTY is present instead of LOCW) except for TYPR with a r of −.20. This reveals that the factors determining the locational behavior of suburbanites may be significantly different than those factors influencing locational behavior for city residents. This, in turn, would necessitate the collection and analysis of a new set of variables for

a. Since the results for the data from rings 1 and 2 is essentially the same as that for all the data, the model results incorporating all the data was used in comparison.

Table 6–17.   Simulation 4: Correlation Matrix for Rings 1 and 2, Milwaukee

	RACE	AGE	OCCUP	MODE	LOCH	LOCW	PCAR	Y	YN	CH	TYPR	SZF
AGE	-0.15											
OCCUP	-0.06	0.11										
MODE	-0.09	-0.05	0.17									
LOCH	-0.34	0.13	0.06	0.13								
LOCW	0.02	0.00	0.15	0.26	0.07							
PCAR	-0.11	0.03	0.04	0.35	0.23	0.13						
Y	-0.08	0.09	0.19	0.17	0.23	0.04	0.39					
YN	-0.58	0.12	0.09	0.15	0.65	-0.02	0.20	0.24				
CH	-0.17	0.15	0.11	0.12	0.30	0.05	0.28	0.70	0.33			
TYPR	0.11	-0.19	-0.07	-0.01	-0.11	-0.11	-0.24	-0.12	-0.09	-0.14		
SZF	0.07	-0.20	-0.07	0.10	-0.08	0.17	0.23	0.10	-0.12	0.07	-0.27	
ACCTY	-0.04	0.04	0.21	0.26	0.16	0.84	0.28	0.42	0.09	0.32	-0.17	0.17

Table 6–18. **Simulation 4: Regression Results for Ring 3, OLS, Milwaukee**

(1) CH = 44.73 + .1657 Y + .0215 YN + 23.28 OCCUP
             (24.63) (.0020)   (.0027)   (14.39)

Standard Deviation = 94.77 R^2 = .9770

(2) LOCH = 5.6788 +   .0001 CH   − .00002 YN − .3821 RACE
              (.2566)   (.0001)   (.8509)

            − .0164 MODE   + .0092 ACCTY
              (.1678)   (.0025)

Standard Deviation = .8439 R^2 = .0700

(3) TYPR = 2.199   −   .0002 CH   − .0624 LOCH −   .0433 SZF
              (.3117)   (.00007)   (.0262)

Standard Deviation = .5959 R^2 = .0772

suburbanites if we are to make meaningful statements about their future movements.

The RACE variable in the second equation has no real content as there are effectively no blacks present in the data. There are also serious multicollinearity problems present particularly between CH and YN (i.e., r of .14 between CH and LOCH whereas r between CH and YN is .45). Finally, the R^2 for this equation for ring 3 data is only .07, which further illustrates its failure as an analyzer and predictor for this particular set of data.

Equation (3) or TYPR, on the other hand, is quite similar for both sets of data with the major differences being the reduced importance of LOCH in determining housing type. This may be due to the fact that most of the units (154 out of 198) are single-family residences and hence the full effect of LOCH on housing type was not reflected as it was when all the data were used, which included a greater percentage of two-family and multi-family structures.

In summary, the regression results for equations (1) and (3) for all three sets of data are quite similar (particularly with respect to the signs of the coefficients) with the only major difference being the more dominant role of income in equation (1) (or CH) for the data from ring 3 versus its role in equation (1) for the regression results based on the data rings 1 and 2 and the regression results based on all the data. The problems arise with the second equation (LOCH variable), which is dramatically different for ring 3 data than it is for either the results for rings 1 and 2 or the results from the entire set of data. This, in turn, may indicate that the locational preferences of suburbanites are dramatically different than those of city dwellers, whereas the way in which they both determine housing expenditures (CH) and housing type (TYPR) are basically the same. Exceptions would include the increased importance of Y in

Table 6–19. Simulation 4: Correlation Matrix for Ring 3, Milwaukee

	RACE	AGE	OCCUP	MODE	LOCH	LOCW	PCAR	Y	YN	CH	TYPR	SZF
AGE	0.04											
MODE	-0.09	0.19										
OCCUP	0.03	-0.13	0.21									
LOCH	-0.04	0.09	0.05	0.04								
LOCW	-0.10	-0.07	-0.04	0.11	0.20							
PCAR	0.07	0.09	0.08	0.38	0.02	0.11						
Y	0.01	0.23	0.23	0.12	0.13	-0.13	0.47					
YN	0.09	0.22	0.20	-0.01	-0.01	0.12	0.17	0.38				
CH	0.01	0.26	0.26	0.13	0.14	-0.14	0.46	0.99	0.45			
TYPR	-0.03	-0.24	-0.12	-0.20	-0.13	-0.02	-0.30	-0.22	-0.16	-0.24		
SZF	0.06	-0.24	-0.01	0.16	0.05	0.09	0.18	0.05	0.02	0.04	-0.13	
ACCTY	0.00	0.08	0.04	0.15	0.29	0.80	0.32	0.36	0.07	0.34	-0.15	0.10

CH for suburbanites and the fact that their stock of housing includes a greater number of single-family residences. In other words, people locate in the suburbs for other important reasons besides their willingness or propensity to spend a greater proportion of their current incomes (than city dwellers) on single-family residences.

Allocation Results from the Regression Models Based on Data from Rings 1 and 2 (City) and Ring 3 Suburb. The purpose here is to examine to what extent the differences in the regression results for the two sets of data will produce different allocational results both in terms of numbers of households per ring and sector and household types—that is, by examining the regression results solely in terms of signs and coefficients, the actual differences between the two sets of data in terms of analysis and prediction might be understated or overstated. Hence, the entire set of data was run through the regression model using the coefficients based on data from rings 1 and 2 (city only) and then all the data was run using the regression results based on data from ring 3 (suburb only).

Table 6–20 presents the results of these two simulation runs (last two columns) as well as the original data allocations and the allocations based on the regression results from the entire set of data (city and suburb). The "city only" model allocates most of the households to ring 2 (i.e., 393 of 581) but also puts a substantial number into rings 1 (102) and 3 (72). In other words, the "city only" model implies that most city dwellers would prefer to live in the outer areas of the city but that due to constraints (e.g., race and income) some will still live in the center city while others are affluent enough to live in the suburbs.

The dramatic difference with the LOCH variable between the "city only" and "suburban only" results is revealed in the allocations projected by the "suburban only" regression coefficients in that they effectively allocate all households to ring 3.

Housing Type. Table 6–21 presents the allocation results of the "city only" and "suburb only" simulations in terms of housing type. The "city only" model reduces the importance of single-family residences in ring 1 from 43 percent of the total stock to 28 percent (79:29 versus 185:102), but increases the importance of two-family residences from 42 percent to 51 percent and multi-family residences from 21 percent to 23 percent. Hence, the model is indicating a slight increase in residential density for ring 1 as compared to the original data. For ring 2, both single-family residences and multi-family residences decline in importance from 43 percent to 35 percent and 12 percent to 4 percent, respectively, whereas two-family residences increase in importance from 45 percent to 61 percent. This implies that the large increase in density in ring 2 would be accommodated in two-family rather than multi-family residences. This,

Table 6–20. Simulation 4: City versus Suburb, Allocation of Households, by Ring and by Sector, Milwaukee

Ring	Sector	Original	Model	City Model Rings 1 and 2	Suburb Model Ring 3
1	1	33	19	20	1
1	2	22	24	24	1
1	3	27	8	8	1
1	4	14	1	1	1
1	5	18	1	17	1
1	6	20	1	3	1
1	7	20	2	15	1
1	8	19	1	5	1
1	9	12 (185)	5 (62)	13 (106)	1 (9)
2	1	22	21	30	1
2	2	22	28	39	1
2	3	22	29	56	1
2	4	22	27	36	1
2	5	22	29	41	1
2	6	22	24	57	1
2	7	22	32	34	1
2	8	22	37	57	1
2	9	22 (198)	27 (254)	43 (393)	1 (9)
3	1	22	37	12	75
3	2	22	14	2	64
3	3	22	34	8	69
3	4	22	30	22	56
3	5	22	32	5	60
3	6	22	39	5	62
3	7	22	30	16	62
3	8	22	25	1	61
3	9	22 (198)	24 (265)	1 (72)	54 (563)

in view of what would happen to land prices as a result of such a dramatic increase in density, does not seem likely. Hence, even when the data is split up such that the data that most powerfully implies single-family residences (i.e., ring 3 data) is not included, the probable increase in multi-family dwellings inhabited is not accurately reflected. This seems to imply the necessity of developing a functional supply constraint (incorporating relative prices), which would indicate that people's housing desires for low-density housing would not be met but rather that their consumer dollars would have to be allocated to more dense housing.

The housing type allocations for ring 3 via the "city only" regression results indicate that single-family residences retain about the same level of importance as they did in the original data (i.e., 77 percent for original data versus 74 percent for "city only"). Two-family residences increase in importance

Table 6–21. Simulation 4: City versus Suburb, Allocation of Households, by Household Type, Milwaukee

Ring	Sector	Single-Family Model	Single-Family City	Single-Family Suburb	Two-Family Model	Two-Family City	Two-Family Suburb	Multi-Family Model	Multi-Family City	Multi-Family Suburb
1	1	3	2	1	10	11	0	6	7	0
1	2	7	19	1	14	3	0	3	2	0
1	3	1	2	1	5	5	0	2	1	0
1	4	0	0	1	1	1	0	0	0	0
1	5	0	0	1	1	12	0	0	5	0
1	6	0	4	1	1	2	0	1	1	0
1	7	0	0	1	0	7	0	1	4	0
1	8	0	0	0	1	3	1	0	2	0
1	9	0 (11)	2 (29)	1 (8)	4 (37)	10 (54)	0 (1)	1 (14)	1 (23)	0 (0)
2	1	7	9	1	12	18	0	2	3	0
2	2	11	17	1	15	19	0	2	3	0
2	3	13	23	1	14	31	0	3	2	0
2	4	9	10	1	15	23	0	4	2	0
2	5	10	17	1	11	23	0	2	3	0
2	6	11	17	1	16	23	0	4	1	0
2	7	12	9	1	18	40	0	3	0	0
2	8	16	23	1	15	30	0	2	1	0
2	9	12 (101)	13 (138)	1 (9)	13 (129)	32 (240)	0 (0)	2 (24)	0 (17)	0 (0)
3	1	30	9	75	7	3	0	0	0	0
3	2	12	1	62	2	1	2	0	0	0
3	3	28	5	69	6	3	0	0	0	0
3	4	28	22	55	2	0	1	0	0	0
3	5	27	3	59	5	2	1	0	0	0
3	6	31	3	62	8	2	0	0	0	0
3	7	25	8	60	5	8	2	0	0	0
3	8	20	1	60	5	0	1	0	0	0
3	9	22 (223)	1 (53)	54 (556)	2 (42)	9 (19)	0 (7)	0 (0)	0 (0)	0 (0)

from 12 percent to 26 percent, which is due to the complete absence of multi-family units in the "city only" allocation.

The "suburb only" regression results not only allocate all families to ring 3 but also effectively place all of them into single-family residences. In addition to its dramatic difference from the "city only" results, it is also interesting to note that no families were allocated to ring 4 (outlying suburbs), which may imply that the families in the proximate, mature suburbs (ring 3) have different preference functions for location than those in ring 4. Perhaps it is those families in ring 4, the newer suburbs, that are the logical extension of the residents in rings 1 and 2 (particularly ring 2) and that the unique group in the urban area is that which first ventured to the suburbs.

Simulation 4: Analysis of Variance for LOCH and TYPR. Table 6–22 presents the analysis of variance about the mean for LOCH and TYPR between the simulation using all the data and the simulating results using the regression coefficients based on the "city only" data. The F-test indicates that both at the .05 and .01 levels, the results are significantly different for both simulations. Similarly, Table 6–23 presents the analysis of variance about the mean for LOCH and TYPR for the simulation using all the data and the simulation results based on the suburb only data. Here too the results are significantly different at both the .05 and .01 levels. Finally Table 6–24 presents the analysis of variance findings for LOCH and TYPR based on a direct comparison between the simulation results for city only and suburb only regression models, which also indicates that at both the .05 and .01 levels the results are significantly different.

Table 6–22. Simulation 4: City versus Suburb, Analysis of Variance for LOCH and TYPR, Rings 1 and 2, or City Results versus Results from Using Model (All Data) Results, Milwaukee

Variable	Source of Variation	Sum of Squares	Degree of Freedom	Mean Square
LOCH	BETWEEN RESULTS	53.1890	1	53.1890
TYPR		4.4243	1	4.4243
LOCH		1629.8000	1160	1.4050
	ERROR			
TYPR		71.8040	1160	.0619
LOCH	TOTAL	1682.9890	1161	
TYPR		76.2283	1161	

F(LOCH) = 37.8577
F(TYPR) = 71.5072
$F_{.05}$ (1,1160) = 3.84[a]
$F_{.01}$ (1,1160) = 6.65

a. Samuel Richmond, *Statistical Analysis*, p. 580.

Table 6–23. Simulation 4: City versus Suburb, Analysis of Variance for LOCH and TYPR, Ring 3, or Suburb Results versus Results from Using Model (All Data) Results, Milwaukee

Variable	Source of Variation	Sum of Squares	Degrees of Freedom	Mean Square
LOCH	BETWEEN RESULTS	259.3699	1	0259.3699
TYPR		12.6516	1	12.6516
LOCH		649.7160	1160	.5601
	ERROR			
TYPR		52.4320	1160	.0452
LOCH	TOTAL	909.1859	1161	
TYPR		65.0836	1161	

F(LOCH) = 463.08
F(TYPR) = 279.83

Table 6–24. Simulation 4: City versus Suburb, Analysis of Variance for LOCH and TYPR, City Results versus Suburb Results, Milwaukee

Variable	Source of Variation	Sum of Squares	Degrees Freedom	Mean Square
LOCH	BETWEEN RESULTS	1830.1868	1	830.1868
TYPE		223.72	1	223.7200
LOCH		1078.2040	1160	.9269
	ERROR		1160	.1670
TYPR		193.72		
LOCH	TOTAL	1908.3908	1161	
TYPR		417.44	1161	

F(LOCH = 896.73
F(TYPR) = 1339.66

Hence, the respective simulation allocations based on the "city only" and suburb only" data bases, as reflected in their regression coefficients, and equation results are significantly different for LOCH and TYPR from the entire data's model allocations and from each other for these two variables.

Chapter Seven

Summary and Conclusions

This summary chapter is divided into three main areas of discussion: (1) general comments on the research; (2) discussion of the signs and coefficients of the individual variables; and (3) discussion of the simulations and some implications of their results.

GENERAL COMMENTS

This research, has attempted to analyze residential location via a demand-oriented, recursive, linear, three equation model. Its variables, as much as possible, had economic content or implications that made the model one of economic location theory. The statistical estimating technique used to generate the parameters was that of ordinary least squares, which technique was in direct correspondence with the recursive nature of the model. The three dependent variables that were generated were CH (annual dollar expenditures on housing), LOCH (linear distance of the residence, from the central business district) and TYPR (the type of residence owned or rented).

The first equation, which analyzed CH, yielded the highest average R^2 (approximately .8 for both Buffalo and Milwaukee), which was basically due to the high significance of current income although the other two independent variables (YN, OCCUP) were also significant for both cities. The performance of this equation is not remarkable as researchers will usually get a relatively high R^2 when analyzing consumption expenditures for housing (or any other consumption good) when current income is included as an independent variable. The contribution of this research is the confirmation of this consumption relationship for individual household's on an intra-and inter-urban basis. The implications of the significance of YN and OCCUP will be discussed further in the next section.

The R^2 for equation two or LOCH varies more widely with a value of .23 for Buffalo and .37 for Milwaukee. The general lower R^2, as compared to equation (1), is due to the greater complexity of the dependent variable. For this equation, there is no independent variable that is as dominant, either theoretically or empirically, as current income is in equation (1). The major independent variables are RACE, YN, and CH, respectively. The contribution of this equation is that it indicates that residential location can be analyzed empirically by using socioeconomic variables, which are themselves significant and which in combination can yield respectable R^2 statistics. Further and perhaps most importantly, this equation indicates that such socioeconomic variables as race and income class clustering have replaced accessibility to work (for the head of the household) as the more significant factors affecting residential location (note: YN and RACE have always been important; it is their relative significance that seems to have risen).

The third equation or the TYPR equation yields the lowest R^2 (.17) for both Buffalo and Milwaukee. This indicates that this linear, socioeconomic approach to the analysis of housing type is not adequate enough or complex enough to reflect the phenomenon of residential housing choice. In this context, it is important to note that this research is only examining a subset of the general urban location phenomenon, which also includes such factors as industrial location, retail location, location of public amenities, and so forth. In examining residential location and housing choice in particular, we are employing the methodological device of "ceteris paribus," which in itself is quite legitimate but may lead to low R^2 for those equations that analyze only a part of a designated subset of urban location, since the dependent variable in these equations may be greatly effected by what has been held constant.

Despite these simplified limitations, equation (3) indicates that location and family size and not just the household budget play significant roles in determining the selection of housing type. The slight dominance of LOCH in both equations reflects the economic result that single-family living can only occur in the outer fringes of urban areas due to the increasingly high cost of land.

SIGNS AND COEFFICIENTS OF THE VARIABLES

First Equation or CH

For equation (1) or CH, the significance and positive sign of the Y variable or current income has already been alluded to and is fairly apparent so it will not be discussed further. The significance for both YN and OCCUP is probably the more interesting finding, particularly for non-aggregated urban households. Their combined significance indicated a substantial ratchet effect for housing consumption, which in turn may imply a permanent income-type consumption relationship.

The significance and positive sign of YN seems to confirm or at least parallel the Duesenberry consumption function that had consumption depending on current income and past peak income, to which behavior Duesenberry gave a socioeconomic interpretation. Basically this interpretation was one in which the consumer would not immediately adjust his current consumption pattern to changes in current income because he was wedded to a consumption pattern based on past peak income. This can also be viewed as immitative consumption behavior based on the income level of one's neighbors (the infamous Joneses) who do not experience the same changes in income. Thus, to the extent that people of the same income class tend to congregate together, as indicated by YN in equation (2), YN may serve as a useful proxy for this economically emulative behavior.

The positive sign and statistical significance of the OCCUP variable as a proxy for expectation of earnings give some credence to the Modigliani concept of the consumption function as one which contains current income as well as an asset variable one of whose components is one's lifetime expectation of earnings. This particular theoretical view of consumption, together with its empirical implications, is particularly crucial for the housing market, which always entails a large outlay of current funds and often is one which involves the purchase (and consumption of services) of a large financial asset.

The actual value of the coefficients for OCCUP were 48.0 for Buffalo and 16.5 for Milwaukee, which is certainly an underestimate of the actual effect of the asset variable, but this is most likely due to the crude proxy value of this variable, which only indicates white-collar or blue-collar employment (with white-collar workers having a higher expectation of earnings).

In short, equation (1) accomplishes the following: (1) confirms the possibility of constructing a housing consumption function for urban residents based on present economic theory; (2) indicates there is a ratchet effect present in this consumption pattern; (3) does not choose an optimum form for the equation but does give some empirical support for variables present in both the Duesenberry and Modigliani functions, which in turn may indicate that the "best" consumption function is a hybird of several proposed functions; (4) can be further refined to give better empirical results particularly with respect to the YN and OCCUP variables (i.e., better proxies can be found).

Second Equation or LOCH

The most important variable, RACE, in the location equation (LOCH) is really a constraint that affects only a particular segment of the entire urban population. It is more significant both statistically and empirically for Buffalo than Milwaukee, but the reasons for the greater importance for Buffalo cannot be determined from presently available data (i.e., employment differences, percentage of population black, and so forth) and information. In any event, its dominance gives credence to the assertions concerning the deleterious effects of racial segregation in terms of limiting housing mobility. Using the findings of equation (1) for blacks only versus the entire data's results (which was biased upwards somewhat due to the presence of the black data), it was estimated that blacks spend from 20 to 30 percent more for housing than do whites of a comparable income level. Further effects of housing segregation will be discussed when the simulation results are summarized.

The YN variable is second in importance in explaining residential location, which indicates that families tend to group together by income class. This variable has greater significance for Milwaukee than Buffalo, which factor, not unlike the RACE variable, is not explicable in that evidence cannot be presented that would indicate why this is so. Perhaps it is related to the average level of median income, which is higher for Milwaukee than Buffalo.

CH is third in importance and its positive sign reflects the notion that people with higher incomes live further out from the central business district, since they have a decided preference for low-density living (i.e., living further out where cheaper land prices exist also enables them to purchase more land). The fact that RACE and YN are more significant than CH indicates that other socioeconomic factors are replacing housing expenditures as the most important locational factor—that is, one must view more factors or variables than just the trade-off between transport costs and site rents when residential location is examined.

This fact is reinforced by the low level of significance attached to the accessibility variables, namely, ACCTY and MODE, which are related to the head of the household's trip. Their combined effect is about half that of either RACE, YN, or CH.

Third Equation or TYPR

The third equation or TYPR revealed that as the independent variables CH, LOCH, and SZF rise in value, there is a tendency for the family to inhabit less-dense housing. The independent variables are approximately equal in importance, but together they yield an R^2 of only .16, which indicates that either more variables need to be added or a different form (non-linear) for the equation should be used or both. In general, the results support the notions that if family housing expenditures grow, size of family increases, or the family moves further out from the CBD, the density of its housing decreases. However, the relatively low levels of the t statistic (i.e., $t \leq 2$) indicate that none of the variables plays a dominant or powerful role in determining housing type. As urban residential patterns become more complex and multi-family dwellings more prevalent and scattered, the difficulty of predicting and analyzing residential location will increase, which implies that the linear form of equation (3) will become even less reliable (i.e., lower R^2). This failure will be enhanced without a functional supply constraint containing relative prices and costs.

IMPLICATIONS AND ANALYSIS
OF SIMULATIONS

Simulation 1: Simple Data Run Using
Regression Coefficients Based on
Respective Data Sets for Milwaukee
and Buffalo

This simulation tested the "goodness of fit" of the respective regression models and also indicated some interesting allocative predictions and insights. For both Buffalo and Milwaukee, this first simulation indicated that only non-whites would inhabit the center city (ring 1), seems to be the direction most center city areas are taking. In general, the model would fail to predict a large influx of wealthy residents to the center city as a result of urban renewal and so forth, since this would reflect a dramatic change from present housing preferences. The model could more successfully reflect this if it were more dynamic in form rather than one of comparative statics. To the extent that housing preferences do not change rapidly over time, the model may be making an additional contribution other than that of indicating that the center city will be dominated by non-whites (which has been asserted by many other researchers); namely, that those who feel that substantial numbers of residents (particularly those of high income) can be lured into the center city may be grossly mistaken.

The white households that were originally allocated to ring 1 are allocated to rings 2 and 3 by the regression models with most going to ring 2. The final net household allocations for rings 2 and 3 are approximately equal in number for Milwaukee, whereas Buffalo gives expressed dominance to ring 2. The Buffalo prediction is the more interesting as it indicates that as households flee the center city for the suburbs, many will not find adequate housing within their budget constraints and may be forced to locate in the outer areas of the city instead.

Despite the significant increases in housing density predicted for rings 2 and 3, the model fails to reflect this via housing type since it does not indicate the requisite increase in multi-family housing. This particular failure can be traced to the absence of a non-functional supply constraint, which would reflect changes in relative costs and prices and hence reallocate households accordingly.

Simulation 2: Change in Income for
Blacks versus Open Occupancy

This simulation indicated that open occupancy was the most effective policy for both Buffalo and Milwaukee for breaking up or dispersing the ghetto. This result was based on the fact that racial segregation rather than insufficient income was the major reason for the concentration of blacks (nonwhites) into a distinctly defined portion of the center of the city.

For Milwaukee, open occupancy was the policy that most effectively reduced housing density due to the real income increase caused by a reduction in the price or cost of housing (i.e., blacks spent a higher percentage of income on comparable housing 20 to 30 percent more than did whites. For Buffalo, the increase in income of $1,000 was more effective in reducing housing density although open occupancy also reduced housing density via the income effect of reduced housing cost.

Since the gap between white and black decreases as income rises (which confirms Becker's findings that middle-income blacks may even spend less for comparable housing than do whites), a possible interpretation of the gap for low-income blacks is that they choose to limit their absolute (but not proportional) expenditures on housing in order to maximize their expenditures on those goods whose consumption is not artificially constrained (e.g., automobiles). If this particular preference function is fairly prevalent, the price of substandard housing will be higher than if their housing preferences more closely paralleled their wealthier counterparts.

Thus, taken together the most effective policy for improving the housing situation for non-whites appears to be a policy of open occupancy rather than income supplements. This conclusion is subject to several qualifications: (1) to the extent that some portion of higher housing prices for non-whites are a result of higher service costs, the income effect of reducing housing price will be lessened because housing prices will not be reduced as much as indicated (i.e., 20 to 30 percent) except for those now paying for costs they do not create; (2) preference functions for housing remain relatively constant; and (3) total utility per consumer is not necessarily highest as a result of open occupancy (this depends on the entire consumer preference map and so forth).

The effectiveness of these two policies both in terms of dispersion of the ghetto and reduction of housing density is overstated because no functional supply constraint was used in conjunction with them—that is, the prices (*ceteris paribus*) that would be paid for housing outside the ghetto as a result of either/or both of these policies will be higher than is implicitly the case in the model due to the increase in price resulting from the increase in quantities demanded of non-ghetto housing.

Simulation 3: Change in Work
Accessibility for Those Employed
in Ring 1

Despite changing work accessibility to ring 1, which was accomplished by halving the distance (time) component of the LOCW variable which in turn affected the accessibility related variable ACCTY (i.e., ACCTY =

LOCW * Y), there was effectively no change in residential location for Buffalo and a slight movement in the wrong direction for Milwaukee (i.e., inward rather than outward). Consequently, this simulation must be considered a partial failure because the effect of such a change in accessibility would undoubtedly be more dramatic although not as significant as some transportation planners would believe. The underestimated allocation results of this simulation can be traced to the following factors: (1) the reflection of the low empirical importance of work accessibility (ACCTY) in equation (2) (LOCH); and the further reduced importance of LOCW in ACCTY; (2) the substitution of distance for time in ACCTY, which works when the transportation network is in an equilibrium state but not in disequilibrium, which this simulation produces by changing the transportation system; and (3) the inability to reflect changes in property values as a result of the change in work accessibility and hence the subsequent adjustments in residential location resulting from such a change.

Simulation 4: Allocation Results Based on Data from Rings 1 and 2 (City) versus Results Based on Data from Ring 3 (Suburbs)

This simulation indicated that the residential preference functions vis-à-vis location (LOCH) are dramatically different for suburbanites (i.e., those living in the older suburbs) than for city dwellers. The implication of this finding is that planners may need to build several models of locational preference for the various subsets of population in an urban area—that is, by making the assumption that suburbanites are simply wealthier city dwellers, they may be grossly mistaken, which will level to serious planning errors if cognizance is not taken of this fact. A further implication of this finding is that residential location becomes a much more complex phenomenon. Not only will we need non-linear, simultaneous models, time series data, more independent variables, particularly supply price related variables, but also a series of models to reflect the different areas and groups in the urban area if meaningful planning and analysis is to be done. In other words, one must build more than one urban model if the predictions of that model depart too drastically from the actions or behavior of the subsets of data that comprise it.

FINAL COMMENTS

In summary, this research has examined residential location behavior on an individual household basis for two cities, Buffalo and Milwaukee. It has provided evidence for a possible housing consumption function using other variables besides current income. A locational function was developed, which yields greater importance for socioeconomic variables than for either work accessibility or housing expenditures. The type of residence inhabited was analyzed via a linear equation that could probably be improved if other variables were available and added (such as relative prices, housing quality, and so forth) and a non-linear form were employed.

The general analysis and predictions of the model would be enhanced if time series data were available and if a functional supply constraint were constructed containing relative prices, costs, and so forth.

In terms of the simulations, evidence was revealed to substantiate the belief that the center city will be inhabited only by non-whites and that whites will continue to flee to the suburbs but many will not make it due to budget constraints, which will confine them to living in the outer areas of the city. Open occupancy was seen to be a very effective policy to simultaneously improve housing location and density for non-whites. Accessibility to work and changes in it do not have a profound effect, via this analysis, on residential location, which is due to its decreased role in residential location as well as the model's static form. Suburbanites were seen to have different locational preferences than city dwellers, which has important implications for future model building, analysis, and predictions.

The simulation results indicate that interesting insights can be gained from this model but that it has definite limitations. This in turn, implies the necessity for constructing a truly dynamic model that would be simultaneous rather than recursive and require historical data for its empirical base.

Notes

CHAPTER ONE
INTRODUCTION

1. For empirical estimation of ACCTY, distance rather than time was used as the two are highly correlated with an R^2 of approximately .9 for many major cities. See Keefer, Louis E. "Vehicle Miles of Travel Accuracy Check," *Interim Technical Report II,* Pittsburgh Area Transportation Study; Mills, Edwin S., "The Value of Land," unpublished Ph.D. dissertation, Johns Hopkins University, 1967; and Pendleton, William "The Value of Highways Accessibility" unpublished Ph.D. dissertation, University of Chicago, 1963.

CHAPTER TWO
URBAN MODEL BUILDING

1. Britton Harriss, "The Uses of Theory in the Simulation of Urban Phenomena," *Journal of the American Institute of Planners,* Vol. 32, No. 5, September 1966, p. 33.
2. Britton Harriss, "Quantitative Models of Urban Development: Their Role in Metropolitan Policy Making," in *Issues in Urban Economics,* edited by Harvey S. Perloff (Johns Hopkins Press, Baltimore, 1968), p. 364.
3. Ibid., p. 371.
4. Ira S. Lowry, "A Short Course in Model Design," *Journal of the American Institute of Planners,* Vol. 31, No. 2, May 1965, p. 364.
5. Britton Harriss, *Issues in Urban Economics,* p. 378.
6. Ira S. Lowry, "Seven Models of Urban Development: A Structural Comparison" (Rand Corporation, Santa Monica, Calif., September 1967).
7. Ibid., pp. 9–11.
8. Ibid., p. 15.

9. Ibid., p. 16.
10. Ibid., p. 15.
11. Ibid., p. 16.
12. Ibid., p. 45.
13. Maurice Kilbridge et al., "A Comparison Framework for Urban Planning Models," Harvard University, Graduate School of Business Administration, Urban Analysis Project, Boston, Mass., January 1968, p. 3.
14. Ibid., p. 7.
15. Ibid., p. 13.

CHAPTER THREE
TWO URBAN MODELS

1. William Alonso, *Location and Land Use* (Harvard University Press, Cambridge, Mass., 1964).
2. Ira S. Lowry, *Model of a Metropolis* (Rand Corporation, Santa Monica, Calif., 1963).
3. William Alonso, *Location and Land Use*, pp. 14–17.
4. Ibid., p. 21.
5. Ibid., pp. 22–24.
6. Ibid., pp. 27–29.
7. E. N. Burgess, "The Determination of Gradients in the Growth of the City," *American Sociological Society Papers* (University of Chicago Press, Chicago, Ill., 1957).
8. Lowdon Wingo, "An Economic Model of the Utilization of Urban Land for Residential Purposes," *Papers and Proceedings of the Regional Science Association*, Vol. 11, 1961, pp. 192–205.
9. Richard Muth, "The Spatial Structure of the Housing Market," *Papers and Proceedings of the Regional Science Association*, Vol. 11, 1961, pp. 206–218.
10. John F. Kain, "Journey to Work as a Determinant of Residential Location," The Rand Corporation, Santa Monica, California, 1961, p. 11.
11. John Meyer, J. F. Kain, and M. Wohl, *The Urban Transportation Problem* (Harvard University Press, Cambridge, Mass., 1966), p. 122.
12. Ibid., p. 139.
13. Ibid., p. 141.
14. Beverly Duncan and Otis Duncan, "The Measurement of Intra-City Location and Residential Patterns," *Journal of Regional Science*, Vol. 2, No. 2, 1960, p. 37.
15. Ibid., p. 45.
16. Ibid., pp. 47–50.
17. Edgar M. Hoover and Raymond Vernon, *Anatomy of a Metropolis* (Harvard University Press, Cambridge, Mass., 1959), p. 132.
18. Richard Muth, "Urban Residential Land and Housing Markets," in *Issues in Urban Economics*, edited by Harvey S. Perloff (Johns Hopkins Press, Baltimore, Md., 1968), pp. 302–3.
19. Ibid., p. 300.
20. Ira S. Lowry, *A Model of a Metropolis*, p. 4.

21. Ibid., p. 5.
22. Ibid., p. 4.
23. Ibid., p. 6.
24. Ibid., pp. 22–23.
25. Ibid., pp. 30–42.
26. Ibid., p. 38.

CHAPTER FOUR
THE BUFFALO MODEL

1. This data was received through the Department of City and Regional Planning, University of North Carolina, at Chapel Hill. They received the data in conjunction with NSF Project GS 1555, which is concerned with the simulation of urban activity patterns.
2. U.S. Bureau of the Census, 1960, Census of Population, Vol. 2, No. 2, Buffalo, N.Y., Department of Commerce, Washington, D.C.
3. All statistical work was done using the statistical package developed by Duke University's Economics Department, which is entitled Program Economics.
4. Carl Christ, *Econometric Models and Methods* (John Wiley and Sons, Inc., New York, 1966), pp. 432–64.
5. Buffalo, Bureau of the Census, p. 42.
6. Margaret Reid, *Housing and Income* (University of Chicago Press, Chicago, Ill., 1962), p. 43.
7. Richard Muth, *Issues in Urban Economics,* p. 285.
8. James Duesenberry, *Income, Saving and the Theory of Consumer Behavior* (Harvard University Press, Cambridge, Mass., 1949).
9. A. Ando, and F. Modigliani, "The Life Cycle Hypothesis of Saving—Aggregate Implications and Tests," *American Economic Review,* Vol. LIII, March 1963.
10. Sherman J. Maisel and Louis Winnick, "Family Housing Expenditures: Elusive Laws and Intrusive Variances," in *Urban Housing,* edited by N. Wheaton et al. (The Free Press, New York, 1966), pp. 150–1.
11. Margaret Reid, *Housing and Income,* pp. 1–40, 372–97.
12. Sherman Maisel, *Urban Housing,* p. 148.
13. Ibid., p. 150.
14. Buffalo, *Census of Population,* p. 48.
15. Sherman Maisel, *Urban Housing,* p. 149.
16. Buffalo, *Census of Population,* p. 49.
17. Gary Becker, *The Economics of Discrimination* (University of Chicago Press, Chicago, Ill., 1957); and Anthony H. Pascal, "The Economics of Housing Segregation," Abstracts of Papers Presented at the December 1965 Meetings, AEA, New York, Econometric Society, p. 2.
18. Britton Harriss, "Quantitative Models of Urban Development: Their Role in Metropolitan Policy Making," in *Issues in Urban Economics,* edited by Harvey S. Perloff (Johns Hopkins Press, Baltimore, Md., 1968), p. 382; and Sherman Maisel, *Urban Housing,* p. 170.

19. Louis E. Keefer, "Vehicle Miles of Travel Accuracy Check," in *Interim Technical Report No. II,* November 1959, for Pittsburgh Area Transportation Study; William Pendleton, "The Value of Highway, Accessibility," unpublished Ph.D. thesis, University of Chicago, 1963, pp. 17–23; and Edwin S. Mills, "The Value of Land," unpublished Ph.D. thesis, Johns Hopkins University, Baltimore, Md., 1967.
20. Sherman Maisel, *Urban Housing,* p. 150.
21. Ibid, p. 148.
22. Britton Harriss, "Uses of Theory in the Simulation of Urban Phenomenon," *Highway Research Record,* No. 126, National Academy of Science, Washington, D.C., 1966, p. 11.
23. R. N. S. Harriss, C. Harrell, and G. S. Tolley, "The Residence Site Choice, *Review of Economics and Statistics,* Vol. 2, No. 2, May 1968, p. 245.
24. Buffalo, *U.S. Census of Population,* 1960.

CHAPTER FIVE
DYNAMIC WORKINGS OF THE BUFFALO MODEL

1. Lionel Needleman, *The Economics of Housing* (Staples Press, London, England, 1965), pp. 45–78.
2. Gary Becker, *The Economics of Discrimination* (University of Chicago Press, Chicago, Ill., 1957), p. 59.
3. Thomas H. Naylor et al., "Methods for Analyzing Data From Computer Simulation Experiments," *Communications of the ACM,* Vol. 10, No. 11, November 1967, pp. 703–10.

CHAPTER SIX
THE MILWAUKEE MODEL

1. The data for the 581 Milwaukee households was obtained through the Southeast Wisconsin Regional Planning Commission, Waukesha, Wisconsin, which data was gathered in 1962 as a part of a Traffic Study conducted by them. This data was supplemented by data from the 1960 Census of Population for Milwaukee.
2. Robert Haughen and A. James Heins, "A Market Separation Theory of Rent Differentials in Metropolitan Areas," *Quarterly Journal of Economics,* November 1969, pp. 660–73.

Bibliography

Alonso, William. *Location and Land Use.* Cambridge, Mass.: Harvard University Press, 1964.

Ando, Anthony and Franco Modigliani. "The Life Cycle of Saving-Aggregate Implications and Tests." *American Economic Review,* VIII (March 1963), 55–85.

Becker, Gary. *The Economics of Discrimination.* Chicago: University of Chicago Press, 1957.

Burgess, E. N. "The Determination of Gradients in the Growth of the City." *American Sociological Society Papers,* Chicago: University of Chicago Press, 1957.

Christ, Carl. *Econometric Models and Methods.* New York: John Wiley & Sons, Inc., 1964.

Duesenberry, James. *Income, Saving and the Theory of Consumer Behavior.* Cambridge, Mass.: Harvard University Press, 1949.

Duncan, Beverly and Otis Duncan. "The Measurement of Intra-City Location and Residential Patterns." *Journal of Regional Sciences,* II (June 1960), 36–55.

Harriss, Britton. "Quantitative Models of Urban Development: Their Role in Metropolitan Policy Making." In *Issues in Urban Economics,* edited by Harvey S. Perloff. Baltimore: Johns Hopkins Press, 1968, 363–413.

_____. "The Uses of Theory in the Simulation of Urban Phenomena." *Journal of the American Institute of Planners,* XXXII (September 1966), 16–35.

_____. "Uses of Theory in the Simulation of Urban Phenomena." *Highway Research Record,* No. 126, 1966, 6–15.

Harriss, R. N. S., C. Harrell, and G. S. Tolley, "The Residence Site Choice." *Review of Economics and Statistics,* II (May 1968), 242–7.

Haughen, Robert and A. James Heins. "A Market Separation Theory of Rent Differentials in Metropolitan Areas," *Quarterly Journal of Economics.* LXXXIII (November 1969), 660–673.

131

Hoover, Edgar and Raymond Vernon. *Anatomy of a Metropolis.* Cambridge, Mass.: Harvard University Press, 1959.

Kain, John F. "Journey to Work as Determinant of Residential Location." Santa Monica: Rand Corporation, 1961.

Keefer, Louis E. "Vehicle Miles of Travel Accuracy Check." *Interim Technical Report II.* Pittsburgh: Pittsburgh Area Transportation Study, 1959.

Kilbridge, Maurice et al. "A Comparison Framework for Urban Planning Models." Cambridge, Mass.: Harvard Business School–Urban Analysis Project, 1968.

Lowry, Ira S. *Model of a Metropolis.* Santa Monica: Rand Corporation, 1963.

_____. "Seven Models of Urban Development: A Structural Comparison." Santa Monica: Rand Corporation, 1967.

_____. "A Short Course in Model Design." *Journal of the American Institute of Planners,* XXXI (May 1965), 92–102.

Maisel, Sherman J. and Louis Winnick, "Family Housing Expenditures: Elusive Laws and Intrusive Variances." In *Urban Housing,* edited by N. Wheaton. New York: Free Press, 1966, 145–75.

Meyer, John, John F. Kain, and Martin Wohl. *The Urban Transportation Problem.* Cambridge, Mass.: Harvard University Press, 1966.

Mills, Edwin S. "The Value of Land." Unpublished Ph.D dissertation, Johns Hopkins University, 1967.

Muth, Richard. "The Spatial Structure of the Housing Market." *Papers and Proceedings of the Regional Science Association,* XI (May 1961), 206–18.

_____. "Urban Residential Land and Housing Markets." In *Issues in Urban Economics,* edited by Harvey S. Perloff. Baltimore: Johns Hopkins Press, 1968, 285–335.

Naylor, Thomas, Kenneth Weitz, and Thomas Wonnacott. "Methods and Analyzing Data from Computer Simulation Experiments." *Communications of the ACM,* X (November 1967), 702–10.

Needleman, Lionel. *The Economics of Housing.* London: Staples Press, 1965.

Pascal, Anthony H. "The Economics of Housing Segregation." Abstracts of Papers Presented at the December 1965 AEA Meetings. New York: AEA, 1965.

Pendleton, William. "The Value of Highway Accessibility." Unpublished Ph.D. dissertation, University of Chicago, 1963.

Reid, Margaret. *Housing and Income.* Chicago: University of Chicago Press, 1962.

Richmond, Samuel. *Statistical Analysis.* New York: Ronald Press, 1965.

U.S. Bureau of the Census, *Census of Population,* 1960, Volume 2, Number 2, Buffalo, New York. Department of Commerce, Washington, D.C.

U.S. Bureau of the Census, *Census of Population,* 1960, Volume 2, Number 2, Milwaukee, Wisconsin. Department of Commerce, Washington, D.C.

Wingo, Lowdon. "An Economic Model of the Utilization of Urban Land for Residential Purposes." *Papers and Proceedings of the Regional Science Association,* XI (May 1961), 195–205.

Index

accessibility: and congestion in simulation, 58; decreasing effect, 125; effect of work on residence, 104; income, distance factors, 67; and location in simulation, 77; role of and amenities, class clustering, 39; and supply constraint, 5

Alonso, William, 15; final market solution, 20

blacks: choice, 68; density, 54; ghetto cohesion, 97; and open occupancy, 75; racial constraints, 71; racial segregation, 124; in simulation, 59; spending power, 103

Buffalo: analysis of model, 53; amenity variable, 45; comparison with Milwaukee, 90; income increase and density, 124; race as a factor, 121; in simulations, 64; statistical model, 30

CBD (central business district): and accessibility, 47; city allocation, 114; core and nonwhites, 126; and density, 75; expressways damage, 77; and household location, 36; immigration, 69; wealthier residents, 123

Chicago: in Kain, 21

city: intra-analysis, 34; market theory, 13; residence pattern, 85; workplace and residential population, 24

construction, 75, 76, 103

consumer: concept of equilibrium, 20

decisionmaking, 53

density: and accessibility, 49; ceiling for residential population in models, 26; increase factors, 66; in Muth, 22; open occupancy, 102; and race, 54; reduction strategy, 124; supply constraint, 5

Detroit: in Kain, 21

Duesenberry, J., 35, 121

Duncan, B. and Duncan, O.D., 22

ethnicity, 54

ghetto: breakup, 97; housing costs, 100; in simulation, 58; strategy, 75

Harris, Britton, 45

homeownership: intermediate steps, 44; and subsidy, 55; value, 34

housing: allocations, 116; amenity variables, 46; blacks, 74; budget constraint, 4; in Buffalo model, 35; consumption function, 121; demand in Lowry, 10; distribution, 66; open occupancy, 75, 98; role of amenities, 39; segregation, 38; segregation and mobility, 121; substitution affects, 45; type, 93–95

income: budget constraints in Alonso, 19; in Buffalo model, 35; class clustering in Milwaukee, 89; and congregation, 38; consumption curve, 45; high and location, 54; in work of Muth, 21; and neighborhood pattern, 43; and open occupancy, 59, 101; subsidy, 75

Kain, John F., 21; on commuting, 43

Kilbridge, M., 13

land: demand surface, 19; demand in work of Lowry, 10; use of in Lowry, 24; value and consumption in work of Alonso, 20

About the Author

Michael Granfield is a graduate of the University of Illinois and Duke University where he received his Ph.D. in Economics. Formerly a professor of Economics with the Graduate School of Management, University of California, Los Angeles, Mr. Granfield subsequently served as Chief Minority Economist with the U.S. Senate Antitrust and Monopoly Subcommittee. He is now with the White House Council in International Economic Policy.